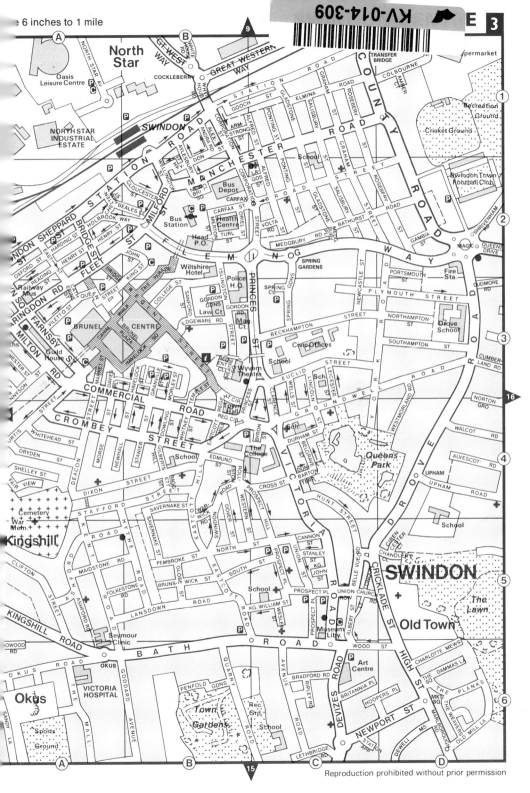

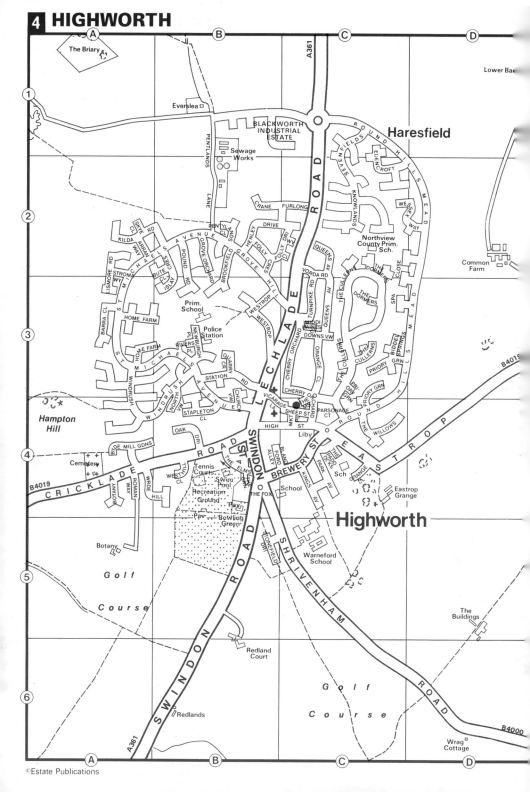

Haresfield

Highworth

The Briary

Everslea

Lower Bar

BLACKWORTH INDUSTRIAL ESTATE

Sewage Works

PENTLANDS LANE

CRANE FURLONG

ROUND HILLS MEAD

SEVENFIELDS

EDEN CROFT

KNOWLANDS

WESSEX WAY

Northview County Prim. Sch.

Common Farm

BENTLANDS CL

HENLEY DRIVE

FOLLY CRES

FOLLY DRI

FCL

QUEENS AV

VORDA RD

THE CULLERNS

THE DORMERS

CLOSE

SKYE RD

ARRAN WAY

KILDA

ISMORE RD

STROMA WY

BUTE CRES

ISLAY

CL

GROVE ORCHARD

BROOMFIELD

POUND RD

GROVE HILL

AVENUE

WESTROP

TURNPIKE RD

QUEENS AV

ORANGE CL

CHERRY ORCHARD

THE DORMERS

SPA

THE CULLERNS

BIDDEL SPRINGS

PRIORY GRN

BARRA CL

HOME FARM

Prim. School

Police Station

WESTROP

MIDDLAINES

DOWNS VW

THE CULLERNS

PRIORY

BIDDEL SPRINGS

HOME FARM

RIVERS PL

NEWBURGH PL

ST MICHAELS

QUARRY CR

CHERRY ORCHARD

CHERRY ORCHARD

PRIORY GRN

WINDRUSH

NORTH

STATION RD

STAPLETON CL

AVENUE

CHURCH

VICARAGE LA

MKT

SHEEP ST

HIGH ST

PARSONAGE CT

THE WILLOWS

LECHLADE ROAD

Hampton Hill

OAK DRI

BE MILL GDNS

Cemetery

WEST HILL CL

WADE HILL

Tennis Courts

THE ELMS

Swim Pool

Recreation Ground

Pav.

Bowling Green

SWINDON ST

BREWERY ST

BLAND FORD ALLEY

PARK AV

KINGS AV

Sch

GRANGE

School

THE FOX

Liby

EAST STROP

Eastrop Grange

BOTANY WY

ROMAN WAY

CRICKLADE ROAD

B4019

Botany

Golf Course

SWINDON ROAD

Redland Court

Redlands

TONEFIELD DRI

SHRIVENHAM

Warneford School

Golf Course

The Buildings

ROAD

B4000

Wrag Cottage

A361

A361

B4019

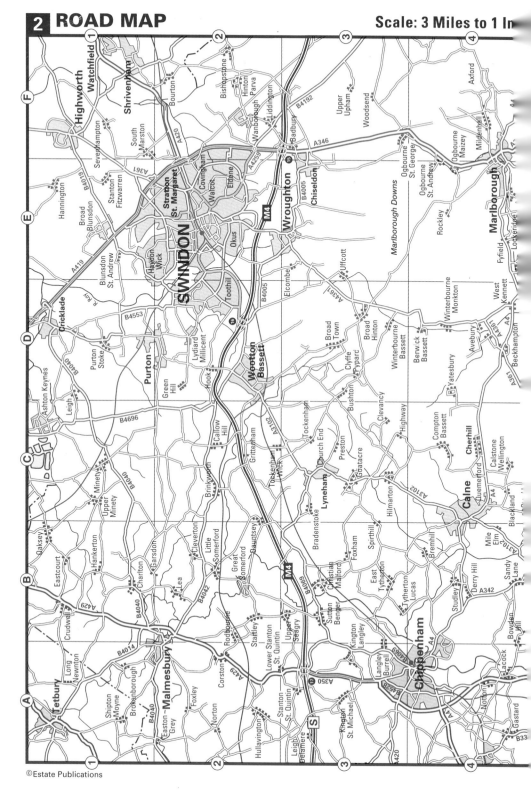

SWINDON · MARLBOROUGH · CHIPPENHAM · WOOTTON BASSETT
CRICKLADE · HIGHWORTH · CALNE · WROUGHTON

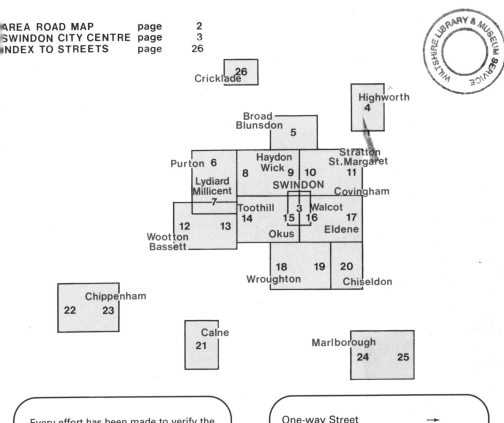

Every effort has been made to verify the accuracy of information in this book but the publishers cannot accept responsibility for expense or loss caused by any error or omission. Information that will be of assistance to the user of the maps will be welcomed.

The representation of a road, track or footpath on the maps in this atlas is no evidence of the existence of a right of way.

Key	
One-way Street	→
Car Park	🅿
Place of Worship	+
Post Office	●
Public Convenience	Ⓒ
Pedestrianized	▨

Scale of street plans: 4 inches to 1 mile
Unless otherwise stated

Street plans prepared and published by ESTATE PUBLICATIONS, Bridewell House, TENTERDEN, KENT, and based upon the ORDNANCE SURVEY mapping with the permission of The Controller of H. M. Stationery Office.

The publishers acknowledge the co-operation of the local authorities of towns represented in this atlas.

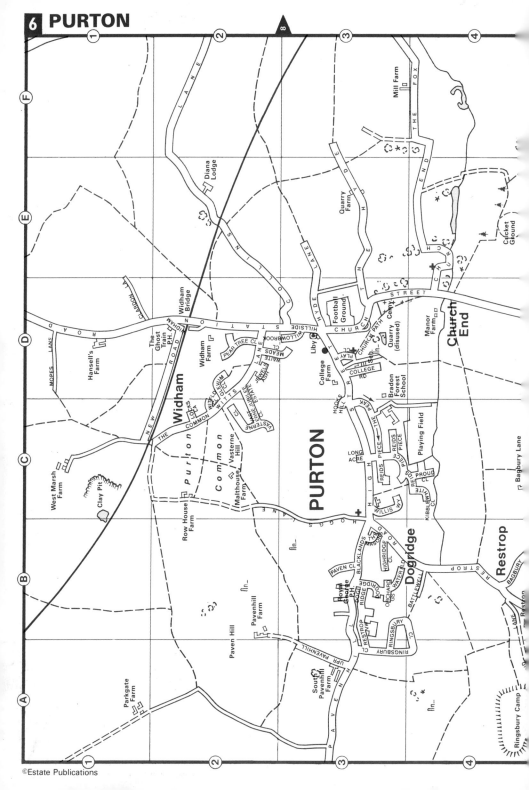

6 PURTON

©Estate Publications

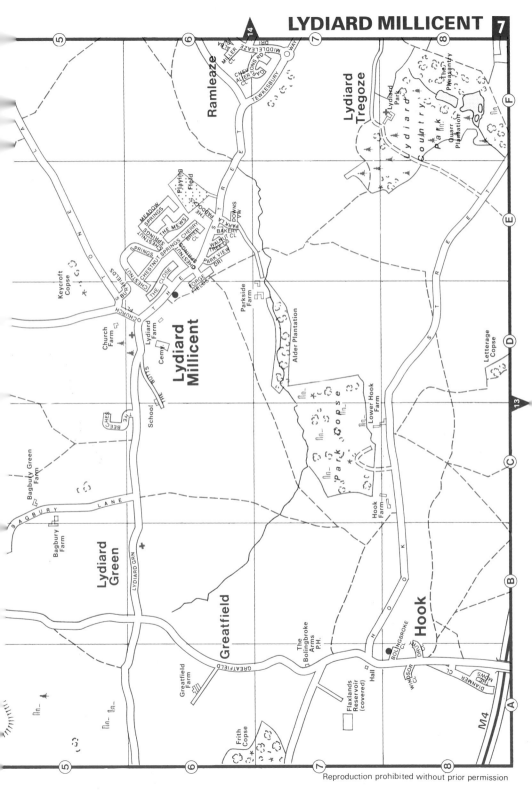

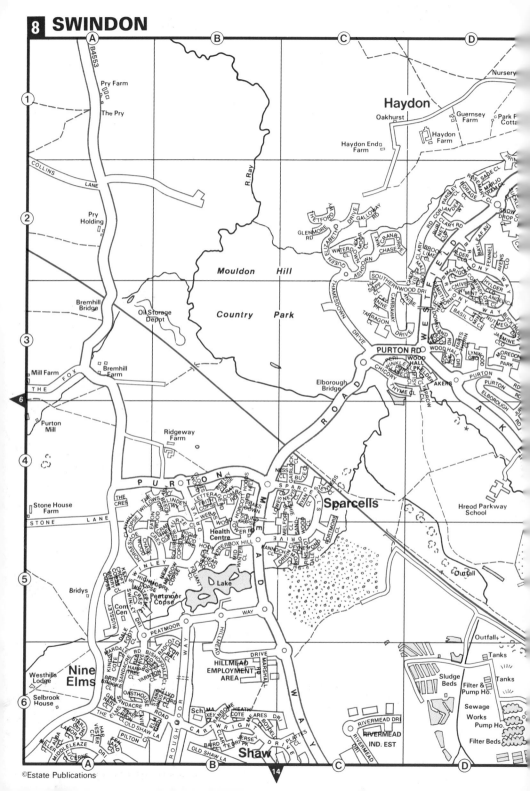

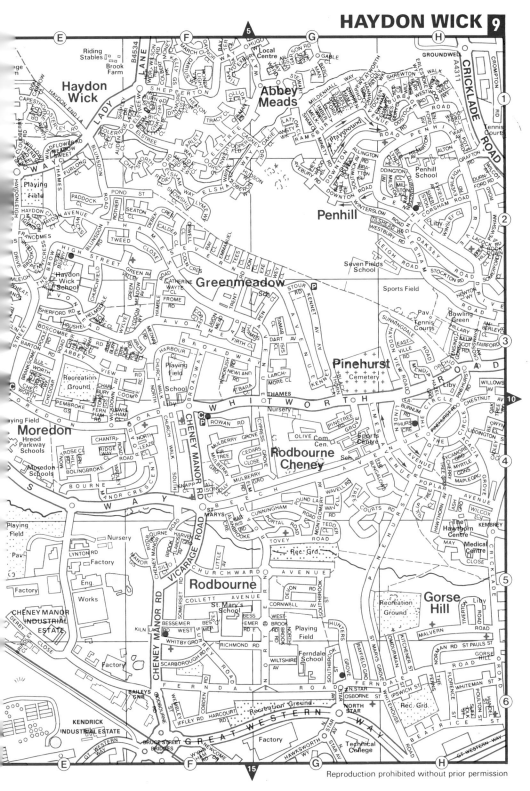

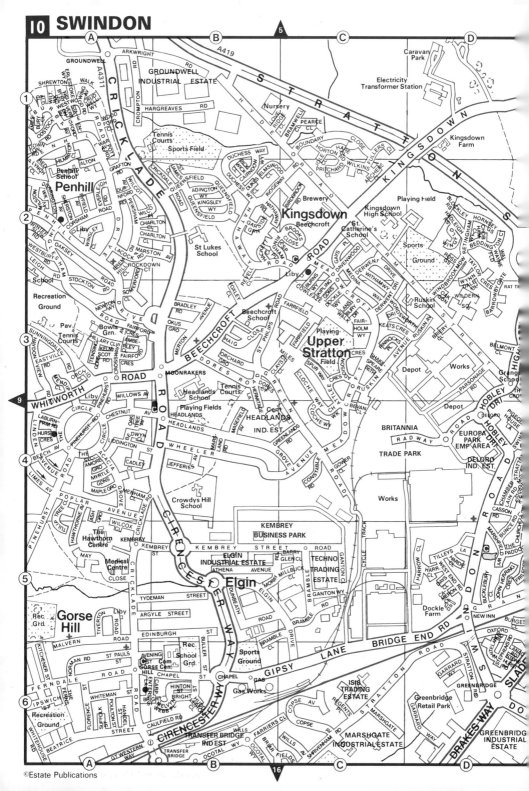

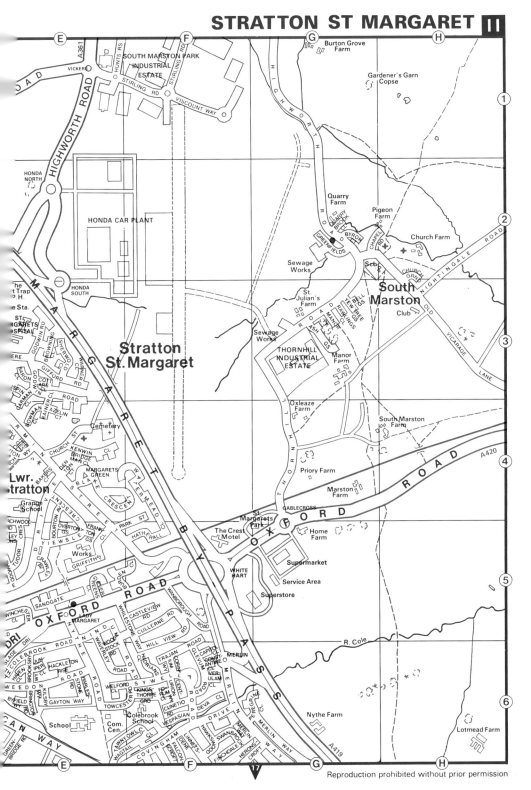

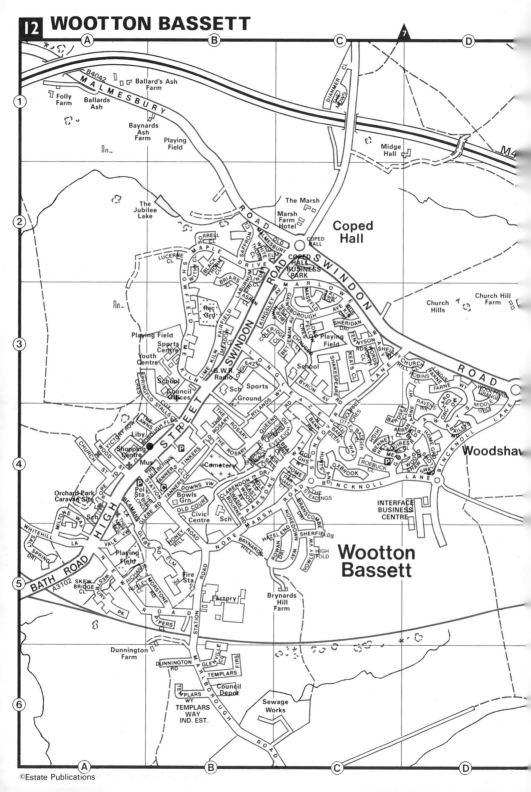

Coped
Hall

Wootton
Bassett

Woodsha

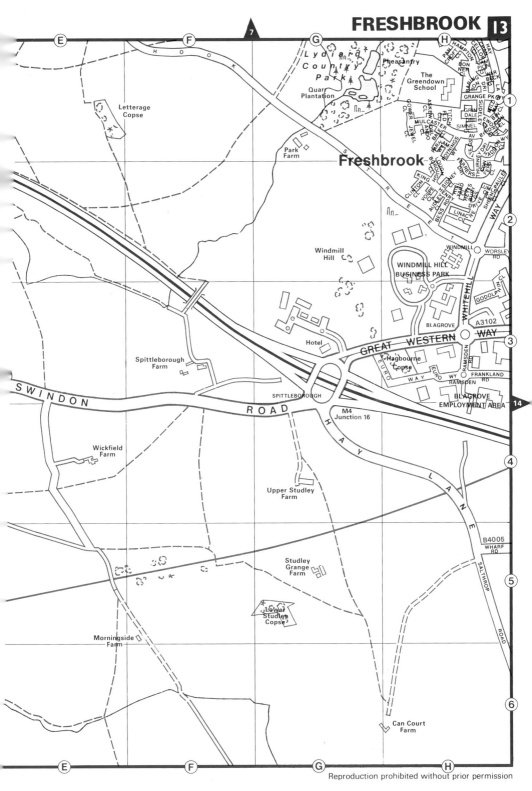

Freshbrook

Lydiard Country Park

Pheasantry

The Greendown School

Quarr Plantation

Letterage Copse

Park Farm

Windmill Hill

Windmill Hill Business Park

WINDMILL

WORSLEY RD

BLAGROVE

A3102

GREAT WESTERN WAY

Hotel

Hagbourne Copse

Spittleborough Farm

SPITTLEBOROUGH

BLAGROVE EMPLOYMENT AREA

FRANKLAND RD

SWINDON ROAD

M4 Junction 16

Wickfield Farm

Upper Studley Farm

HAY LANE

B4005 WHARF RD

Studley Grange Farm

SALTHROP ROAD

Lower Studley Copse

Morningside Farm

Can Court Farm

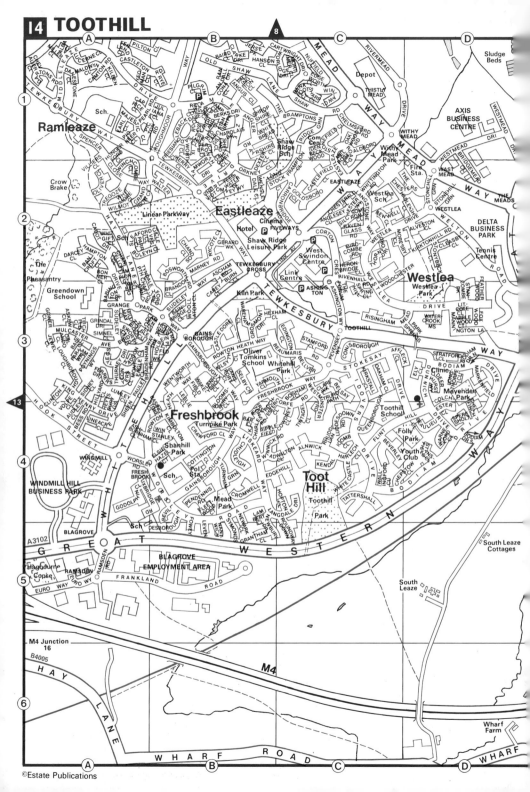

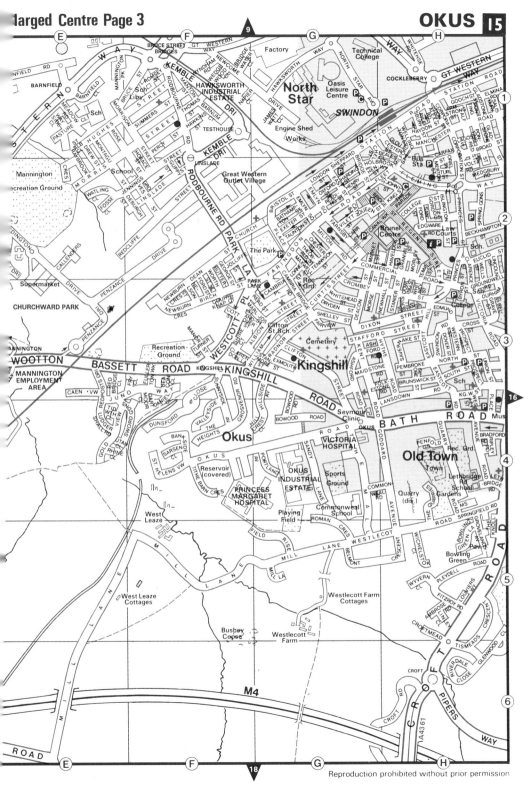

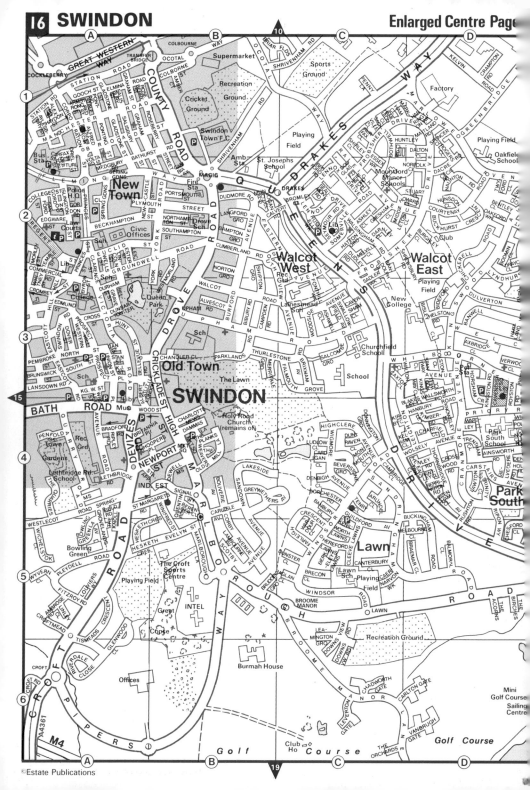

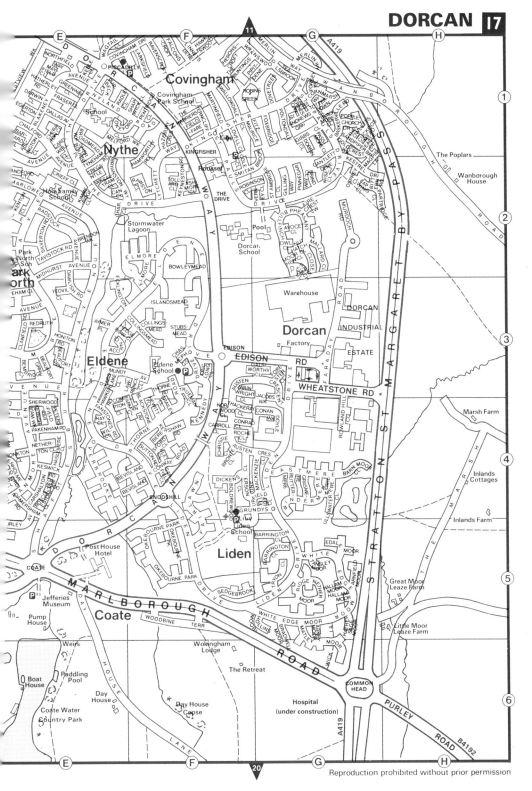

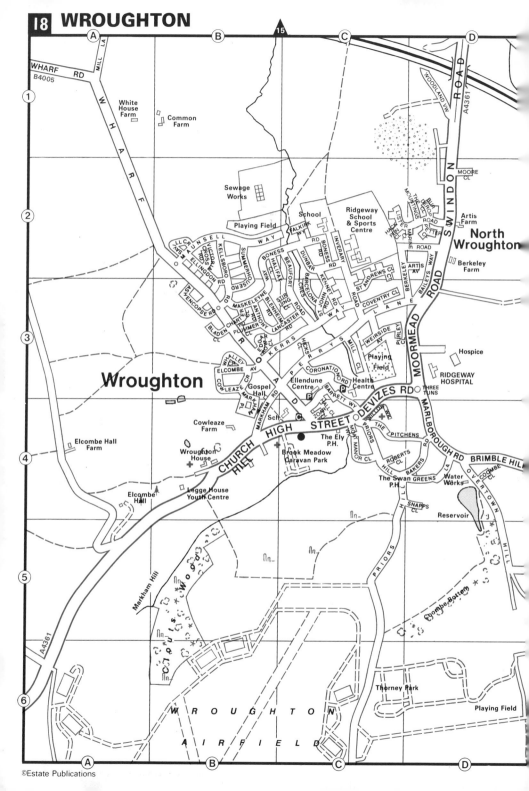

18 WROUGHTON

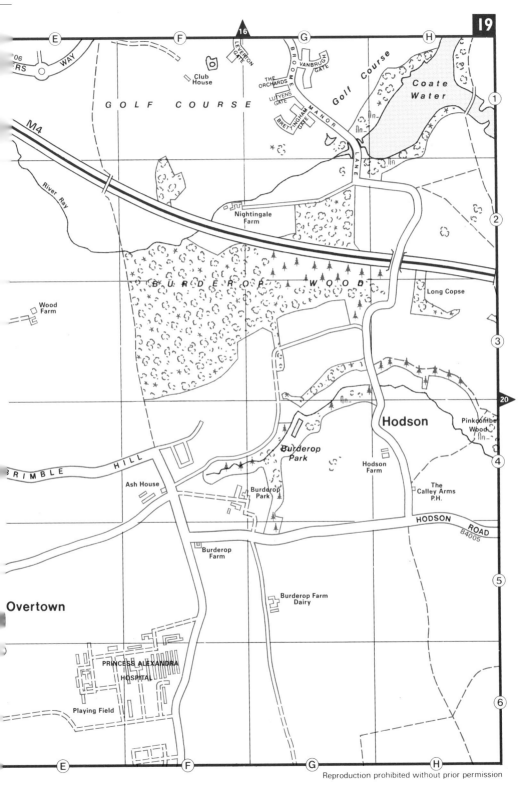

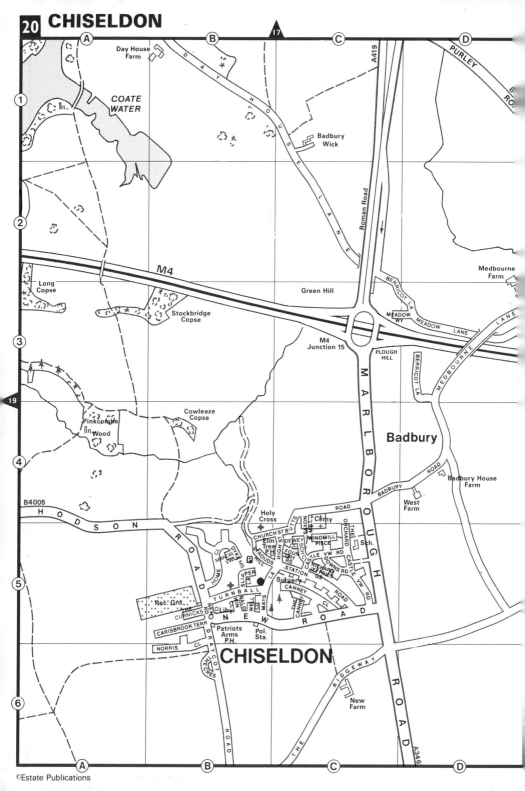

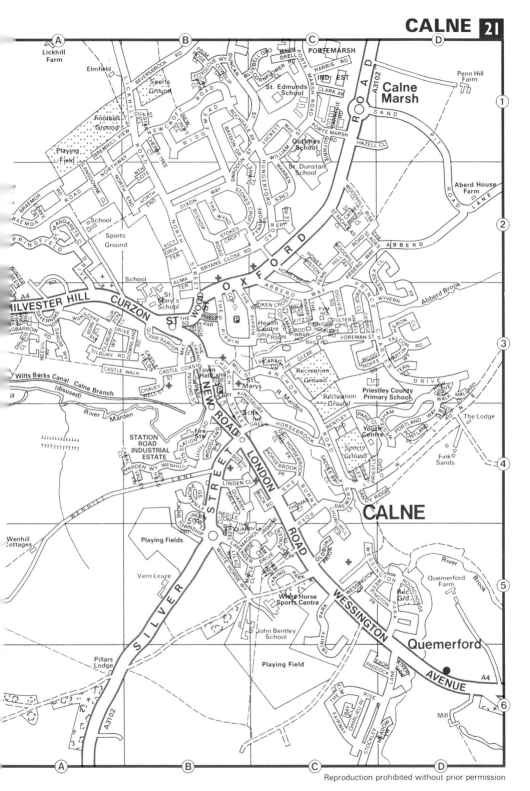

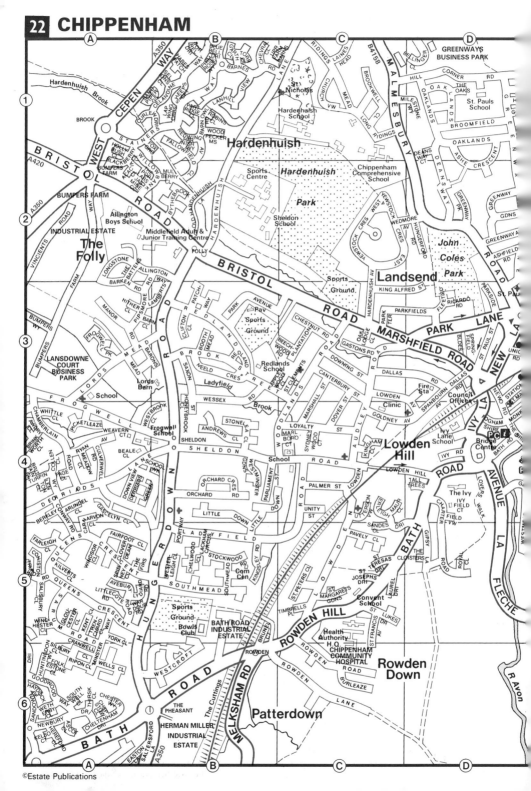

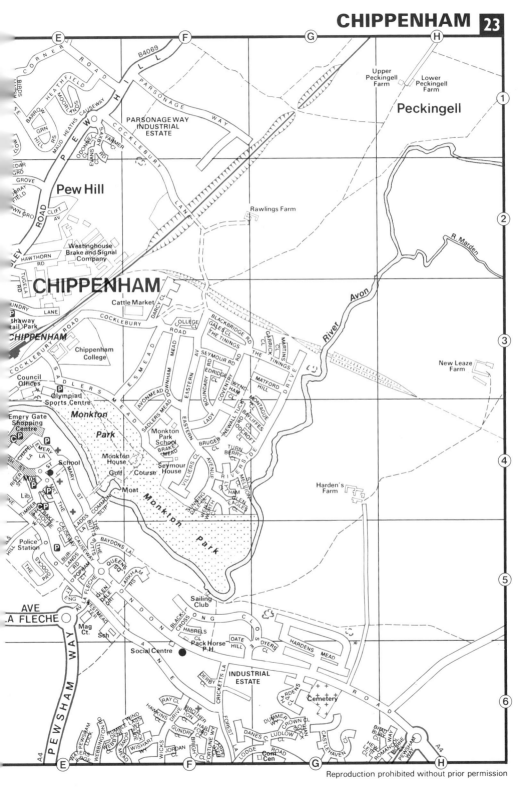

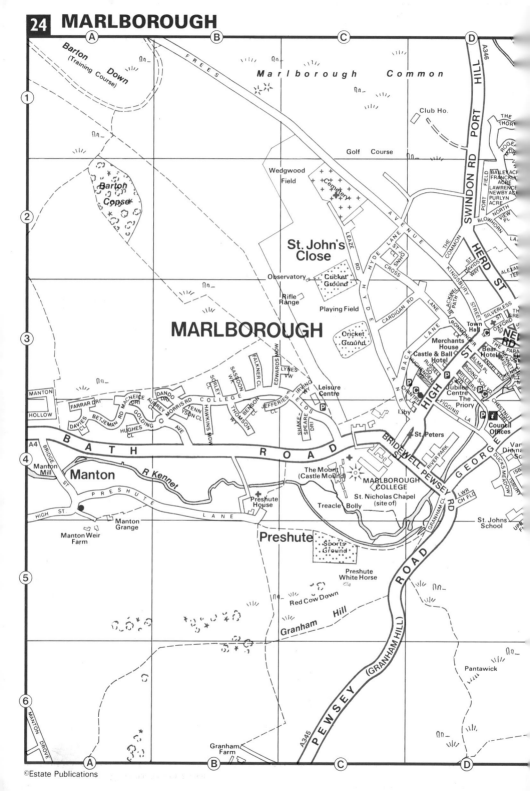

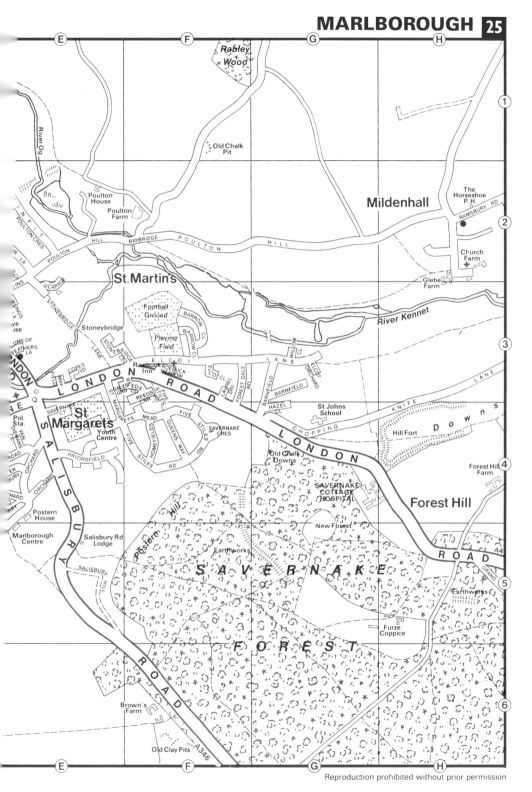

Elsie Hazel Ct. SN5 14 B4
Elstree Way. SN2 9 F1
Ely Clo. SN5 14 D3
Emlyn Sq. SN1 3 A3
Emmanuel Clo. SN2 9 F2
Enford Av. SN2 9 H1
Ensor Clo. SN2 5 C3
Eric Long Clo. SN3 17 F3
Erlestoke Way. SN2 9 H1
Ermin St. SN2 5 C2
Ermin St. SN3 10 C2
Espringham Pl. SN2 10 B2
Essex Walk. SN2 16 C2
Euclid St. SN1 3 C3
Euro Way. SN5 14 A5
Europa Pk Employment
 Area. SN3 10 D3
Evelyn St. SN3 16 B5
Evergreens Clo. SN3 11 E5
Everleigh Rd. SN2 9 H2
Eworth Clo. SN5 14 A3
Exbury Clo. SN2 9 F1
Exe Clo. SN2 9 G2
Exeter St. SN1 15 G2
Exmoor Clo. SN2 8 C2
Exmouth St. SN1 15 G3

Fairfax Clo. SN3 16 C1
Fairford Cres. SN2 9 H3
Fairholme Way. SN2 10 C3
Fairlawn. SN3 17 F5
Fairview. SN1 3 A4
Falconscroft. SN3 17 F1
Falmouth Gro. SN3 16 C3
Fanstones Rd. SN3 17 E4
Faraday Rd. SN3 17 G3
Fareham Clo. SN3 17 E3
Farleigh Cres. SN3 16 C5
Farman Clo. SN3 17 F4
Farnborough Rd. SN3 16 D5
Farnsby St. SN1 3 A3
Farrfield. SN2 10 C3
Farriers Clo. SN1 10 B6
Feather Wood. SN5 14 D3
Fenland Clo. SN5 14 A1
Fennel Clo. SN2 8 D2
Ferndale Rd. SN2 9 F6
Fernham Rd. SN2 9 E4
Ferrers Dri. SN5 14 A3
Field Rise. SN1 15 G5
Fieldfare. SN3 17 F1
Finchdale. SN3 11 F6
Fir Tree Clo. SN2 9 F4
Firecrest Vw. SN3 17 G2
Firth Clo. SN2 9 F3
Fitzmaurice Clo. SN3 17 F1
Fitzroy Rd. SN1 16 A5
Fleet St. SN1 3 A2
Fleetwood Ct. SN5 14 B4
Fleming Way. SN1 3 B2
Flint Hill. SN5 14 C4
Florence St. SN2 9 H6
Folkestone Rd. SN1 3 A5
Fonthill Walk. SN3 16 C3
Ford St. SN1 15 F3
Forester Clo. SN3 17 G3
Forge Fields. SN5 7 D6
Forsey Clo. SN3 17 G1
Forum Clo. SN3 11 F6
Fosse Clo. SN2 15 E2
Fouant Clo. SN5 8 B5
Fowey. SN5 14 B4
Fox Hill Clo. SN2 9 F3
Fox Wood. SN5 14 D3
Foxbridge. SN3 17 G1
Foxglove Rd. SN2 8 D2
Foxley Clo. SN2 10 B3
Frampton Clo. SN5 14 C2
Francomes. SN2 9 E2
Frankland Rd. SN5 14 A5
Frankton Gdns. SN3 11 E5
Fraser Clo. SN3 17 E1
Freshbrook Way. SN5 14 B3
Friesland Clo. SN5 14 B1
Friesian Clo. SN5 14 B1
Frilford Dri. SN3 10 D5
Frith Copse. SN5 8 B4
Frobisher Dri. SN3 16 C2
Frome Rd. SN2 9 F3
Fry Clo. SN5 15 F3
Fuller Clo. SN2 10 C2
Fullerton Walk. SN5 15 F3
Furlong Clo. SN2 9 E2
Furze Clo. SN5 8 B4

Fyfield Av. SN2 9 H2
Fyne Clo. SN5 8 C5

Gable Clo. SN2 9 G1
Gainsborough Way. SN5 14 B4
Gairlock Clo. SN5 8 C4
Galloway Clo. SN5 14 B1
Galloway Rd. SN2 8 C2
Galsworthy Clo. SN3 17 G3
Gambia St. SN1 3 D2
Gantlett Dene. SN3 17 G2
Ganton Clo. SN2 10 C5
Ganton Way. SN2 10 C5
Garfield Clo. SN3 17 F4
Garrard Way. SN3 10 D6
Garside Grn. SN2 10 B2
Garson Rd. SN2 9 G1
Gartons Rd. SN5 14 A1
Gaynor Clo. SN2 9 F1
Gays Pl. SN2 10 C2
Gayton Way. SN3 11 E6
George St. SN1 15 F2
Gerard Walk. SN5 14 B2
Gibbs Clo. SN3 17 G1
Gifford Rd. SN3 11 E3
Gilberts Hill. SN1 3 B4
Gilham Clo. SN2 5 C3
Gilling Way. SN3 17 G2
Gipsy La. SN2 10 B6
Gladstone St. SN1 3 C1
Glenmore Rd. SN2 8 C2
Glenwood Clo. SN1 16 A6
Glevum Clo. SN5 6 D2
Glevum Rd. SN3 11 F6
Globe St. SN1 3 B5
Gloucester St. SN1 3 B2
Goddard Av. SN1 3 A6
Godolphin Clo. SN5 14 A4
Godwin Rd. SN3 11 E3
Gold View. SN5 15 E4
Goldcrest Walk. SN3 17 G1
Goldsborough Clo. SN5 14 C2
Gooch St. SN1 3 B1
Gordon Gdns. SN1 3 B3
Gordon Rd. SN1 3 B3
*Gore Clo,
 Hepworth Rd. SN2 9 F1
Goulding Clo. SN3 10 D4
Gower Clo. SN5 14 A3
Gower Clo. SN2 10 C4
Grafton Rd. SN2 10 A2
Graham St. SN1 3 C1
Grailey Clo. SN3 17 F4
Granary Clo. SN5 8 A6
Grandison Clo. SN5 14 A2
Grange Dri. SN3 10 D5
Grange Park Way. SN5 14 A3
Grantham Clo. SN5 14 B5
Grantley Clo. SN3 16 D4
Granville St. SN3 11 B3
Grasmere. SN3 17 G4
Graythwaite Clo. SN3 9 F1
Great Western Way. SN5 14 A5
Greatfield. SN4 7 A6
Green Hill Rd. SN2 9 E4
Green Meadow Av. SN2 9 F3
Green Rd. SN2 10 B3
Green Valley Av. SN2 9 F2
Greenbridge Ind Est. SN3 10 D6
Greenbridge Retail Pk. SN3 10 D6
Greenbridge Rd. SN3 16 D1
Greenfields. SN3 11 G2
Greenlands Rd. SN2 10 C4
*Greensand Clo,
 W. Highland Av. SN2 5 B4
Greenway Clo. SN3 17 E1
Greenwich Clo. SN2 9 F2
Gresham Clo. SN3 16 C2
Greywethers Av. SN3 16 B4
Griffiths Clo. SN3 11 E5
Grindall Dri. SN5 14 A3
Grosmont Dri. SN5 14 B3
Grosvenor Rd. SN1 15 F4
Groundwell Ind Est. SN2 10 B1
Groundwell Rd. SN1 3 C4
Grovelands Av. SN1 16 A5
Groves St. SN2 15 F2
Grundys. SN3 17 F4
Guildford Av. SN3 16 C5
Guppy St. SN2 15 F2
Hackett Clo. SN2 10 B2

Hackleton Rise. SN3 11 E6
Haddon Clo. SN5 14 A3
Hadleigh Clo. SN5 14 D2
Hadleigh Rise. SN3 10 D2
Hadrians Clo. SN3 11 F6
Haig Clo. SN2 10 B3
Hallam Moor. SN3 17 G5
Hamble Rd. SN2 9 F3
Hamilton Clo. SN3 16 C1
Hampshire Clo. SN5 14 B1
Hampton Dri. SN5 14 A2
Hamstead Way. SN2 5 C4
Hamworthy Rd. SN3 17 F2
Hanbury Rd. SN3 16 D4
Handel St. SN2 9 H6
Hannington Clo. SN2 9 G1
Hanson Clo. SN5 14 B1
Harbour Clo. SN2 9 F3
Harcourt Rd. SN2 9 F6
Hardie St. SN1 3 A2
Hardwick Clo. SN2 9 F2
Hare Clo. SN2 10 C1
Harebell Clo. SN2 9 E2
Harlech Clo. SN5 14 C4
Harlestone Rd. SN3 11 E6
Harptree Clo. SN5 8 A6
Harrington Walk. SN3 16 D1
Harris Rd. SN2 9 F5
Harrow Clo. SN3 10 D5
Hartland Clo. SN3 16 D3
Hartsthorn Clo. SN2 8 D3
Harvester Clo. SN5 8 A6
Harvey Gro. SN2 9 F5
Haslemere Clo. SN3 17 E4
Hatchers Cres. SN3 5 D2
Hatfield Clo. SN2 9 E1
Hathaway Rd. SN2 10 B2
Hatherall Clo. SN3 11 F5
Hatherley Rd. SN3 17 E1
Hathersage Moor. SN3 17 G5
Hatton Gro. SN3 16 C2
Havelock Sq. SN1 3 B3
Havelock St. SN1 3 B3
Haven Clo. SN3 11 E6
Hawker Rd. SN3 17 E3
Hawkfinch Clo. SN3 17 G2
Hawkins St. SN2 15 F1
Hawkswood. SN3 17 F4
Hawksworth Ind Est.
 SN2 15 F1
Hawksworth Way. SN2 15 G1
Hawthorn Av. SN2 9 H4
Hay La. SN4 14 A6
Haydon Clo. SN2 9 E2
Haydon Ct Dri. SN2 9 E2
Haydon End La. SN2 9 E1
Haydon St. SN1 3 B2
Haydon View Rd. SN2 9 H3
Haydonleigh Dri. SN2 9 E2
Haynes Clo. SN3 17 E4
Hayward Clo. SN2 9 G1
Hazebury Cres. SN3 17 F1
Hazel Gro. SN2 9 H3
Headlands Gro. SN2 10 B4
Headlands Ind Est. SN2 10 B4
Heath Way. SN3 11 E6
Heathcote Clo. SN5 8 B6
Heaton Clo. SN2 9 F1
Heddington Clo. SN2 9 H2
Hedgerow Clo. SN3 17 E3
Hedges Clo. SN3 11 E4
Helmsdale. SN2 9 E3
Helston Rd. SN3 16 D3
Henley Rd. SN3 16 D4
Henry St. SN1 3 A2
Hepworth Rd. SN2 9 F1
Hereford Lawns. SN3 16 C5
Hermitage La. SN2 10 B3
Heronbridge Clo. SN5 14 C2
Heronscroft. SN3 17 F1
Hertford Clo. SN3 16 C2
Hesketh Cres. SN3 16 A5
Hewitt Clo. SN3 17 F4
Hexham Clo. SN5 14 B3
Heytsbury Gdns. SN5 14 A4
Heywood Clo. SN3 9 G2
High Rd. SN2 5 D2
High St,
 Broad Blunsdon. SN2 5 D2
High St,
 Chiseldon. SN4 20 C5
High St,
 Haydon Wick. SN2 9 E2
High St, Purton. SN5 6 C3

High St, Swindon
 Old Town. SN1 3 D6
Highclere Av. SN3 16 C4
Highdown Way. SN2 5 C4
Highland Clo. SN5 14 B1
Highmoor Copse. SN5 8 A5
Hignham Clo. SN3 10 D5
Highridge Clo. SN5 6 B3
Highwood Clo. SN2 8 D3
Highworth Rd. SN3 10 D3
Hill View Rd. SN3 11 F6
Hillary Clo. SN2 9 H3
Hillcrest Clo. SN1 15 G4
Hillingdon Rd. SN3 17 E4
Hillmead Dri. SN5 8 B5
Hillmead Employment
 Area. SN5 8 B6
Hillside. SN5 6 D3
Hillside Av. SN1 15 G4
Hillside Clo. SN1 15 G4
Hillside Way. SN2 5 C2
Hillyard Clo. SN5 14 A3
Hilmarton Av. SN2 9 H1
Hinkson Clo. SN2 5 B3
Hinton St. SN2 10 B6
Hobley Dri. SN3 10 D4
Hodds Hill. SN5 8 B4
Hodson Rd. SN4 20 A4
Hogs La. SN5 6 B3
Holbein Field. SN5 14 B3
Holbein Mews. SN5 14 B3
Holbein Pl. SN5 14 B3
Holbein Walk. SN5 14 B3
Holbrook Way. SN1 3 A2
Holdcroft Clo. SN2 5 D2
Holden Cres. SN2 9 G1
Holinshed Pl. SN5 14 B3
Holliday Clo. SN2 9 F1
Hollins Moor. SN3 17 G5
Holly Clo. SN2 9 F4
Holmleigh. SN2 9 E3
Home Clo. SN4 20 B5
Honda Car Plant. SN3 11 E2
Honeylight Vw. SN2 9 F1
Honeysuckle Clo. SN2 8 D3
Honiton Rd. SN3 17 E3
Hook Clo. SN5 8 B5
Hook St. SN4 7 B7
Hooks Hill. SN5 6 C3
Hoopers Pl. SN1 3 C6
Hopton Clo. SN5 14 C4
Horace St. SN2 15 F2
Horcot Rd. SN5 8 B4
Hornsey Gdns. SN3 10 D2
Horseshoe Cres. SN5 8 A5
Horsham Cres. SN3 16 D3
Horton Rd. SN2 10 C1
Howard Clo. SN3 16 C2
Huddleston Clo. SN2 10 B6
Hudson Way. SN2 9 F2
Hughes St. SN2 15 E1
Hugo Way. SN2 9 F2
Hungerford Clo. SN5 14 A1
Hunsdon Clo. SN5 16 D2
Hunt St. SN1 3 C4
Hunters Gro. SN2 9 G5
Huntley Clo. SN3 16 C1
Hunts Hill. SN2 5 D2
Hunts Rise. SN3 11 E1
Hurst Cres. SN2 9 H4
Hyde La. SN5 6 D3
Hyde Rd. SN2 10 B1
Hylder Clo. SN2 8 D3
Hysopp Clo. SN2 8 C3
Hythe Rd. SN1 3 B5

Icomb Clo. SN5 14 C4
Idovers Dri. SN5 14 C3
Iffley Rd. SN2 9 F6
Imber Walk. SN2 9 G1
INDUSTRIAL ESTATES:
Axis Business Centre.
 SM5 14 D1
Blagrove Employment
 Area. SN5 14 A5
Britannia Trade Pk.
 SN3 10 C4
Cheney Manor
 Ind Est. SN2 9 E5
Churchward Pk. SN5 15 E3
Deloro Ind Est. SN3 10 B5
Delta Business Pk.
 SN5 14 D2
Dorcan Ind Est. SN3 17 G3
Elgin Ind Est. SN2 10 B5
Europa Pk Employment
 Area. SN3 10 D4

Greenbridge Ind Est.
 SN3 10 D...
Greenbridge
 Retail Pk. SN3 10 D...
Groundwell Ind Est.
 SN2 10 B...
Hawksworth Ind Est.
 SN2 15 F...
Headlands Ind Est. SN2 10 B4
Hillmead Employment
 Area. SN5 8 B6
Honda Car Plant. SN3 11 E2
Isis Trading Est. SN1 10 C6
Kembrey
 Business Pk. SN2 10 B5
Kendrick Ind Est. SN2 9 E6
Mannington Employment
 Area. SN5 15 E3
Marshgate Ind Est.
 SN1 10 C6
Okus Ind Est. SN1 15 G4
Rivermead Ind Est.
 SN5 8 C6
South Marston
 Park Ind Est. SN3 11 F1
Stratton Road
 Ind Est. SN2 10 C6
Techno Trading Est.
 SN2 10 C5
Thornhill Ind Est. SN3 11 G3
Transfer Bridge Ind Est.
 SN1 10 B6
Westmead Ind Est.
 SN5 14 D1
Windmill Hill
 Business Pk. SN5 14 A4
Inglesham Rd. SN2 9 H2
Ipswich St. SN2 9 H6
Irston Way. SN5 14 B4
Isis Clo. SN2 9 G3
Isis Trading Est. SN1 10 C6
Islandsmead. SN3 17 F3
Islington St. SN1 3 B2
Ivy La. SN2 5 D1
Ixworth Clo. SN5 14 B1

*Jack Thorne Clo,
 Linden Way. SN5 8 B4
Jacobs Walk. SN3 17 G3
James Watt Clo. SN2 15 F1
Jasmine Clo. SN2 8 D3
Jefferies Av. SN2 10 B4
Jennings St. SN2 15 F2
Jersey Pk. SN5 14 B1
Jewel Clo. SN5 14 A3
Jewels Ash. SN5 6 D2
John Herring Cres. SN3 10 D5
John St. SN1 3 B2
Jole Clo. SN2 10 C2
Jolliffe St. SN1 15 F2
Joseph St. SN1 15 G3
Joyce Clo. SN2 5 C4
Jubilee St. SN5 6 D2
Jubilee Rd. SN2 8 D4
Juliana Clo. SN5 14 B1
Juniper Clo. SN3 11 E6
Juno Way. SN5 15 E3

Karslake Clo. SN3 17 E3
Keats Cres. SN3 10 C3
Keble Clo. SN3 17 E1
Kelham Clo. SN3 16 C4
Kelly Gdns. SN2 9 F1
Kelmscot Rd. SN3 9 H3
Kelvin Rd. SN3 16 D1
Kemble Dri. SN2 15 F1
Kembrey Business Pk.
 SN2 10 B5
Kendal. SN3 14 C4
Kendrick Ind Est. SN2 9 E6
Kenilworth Lawns. SN3 16 C5
Kennedy Dri. SN3 17 F4
Kennet Av. SN2 9 G3
Kent Rd. SN1 3 A5
Kenton Clo. SN3 17 E2
Kenwin Clo. SN3 11 E4
Kerry Clo. SN5 14 B2
Kestrel Dri. SN3 17 G2
Keswick Rd. SN3 17 E4
Keycroft Copse. SN5 8 A5
Keyneston Rd. SN3 17 E2
Keynsham Walk. SN3 17 E4

ibblewhite Clo. SN5 6 C4
Kilben Clo. SN5 14 A1
Kiln La. SN. SN2 9 F5
Kilsby Way. SN5 11 E6
Kilsyth Clo. SN5 14 B3
Kimberley Rd. SN3 16 D4
Kimbolton Clo. SN5 14 B4
Kimmeridge Clo. SN3 17 E2
King Charles Rd. SN5 14 B4
King Henry Dri. SN5 14 A3
King John St. SN1 3 C5
King St. SN1 3 B2
King William St. SN1 3 C5
Kingfisher Dri. SN3 17 F1
Kingscote Clo. SN5 8 A6
Kingsdown La. SN2 5 E3
Kingsdown Rd. SN2 10 C2
Kingshill Rd. SN1 3 A5
Kingsley Way. SN2 10 B2
Kingsthorpe Gro. SN3 11 F6
Kingston Rd. SN3 16 D4
Kingsway Clo. SN3 16 D3
Kingswood Av. SN3 16 D3
Kipling Gdns. SN2 10 C3
Kirby Clo. SN3 16 C4
Kirkstall Clo. SN5 14 C3
Kirktonhill Rd. SN5 14 D2
Kitchener St. SN2 9 H6
Knapp Clo. SN2 9 F4
Knowsley Rd. SN3 16 D4

Laburnum Rd. SN2 9 H4
Lacock Rd. SN2 10 A2
Lady La. SN3 5 C3
Lagos St. SN1 3 C2
Lakeside. SN3 16 B4
Lambert Clo. SN5 14 B6
Lambourne Av. SN3 16 B5
Lamora Clo. SN5 8 A6
Lanac Rd. SN3 10 D6
Landor Rd. SN2 5 B5
Langdale Dri. SN3 14 B4
Langford Gro. SN3 16 B2
Langport Clo. SN5 14 B3
Langstone Way. SN5 14 C2
Lanhydrock Clo. SN5 14 B3
Lansbury Dri. SN2 10 C3
Lansdown Rd. SN1 3 B5
Lapwing Clo. SN3 17 G2
Larchmore Clo. SN2 9 G3
Larksfield. SN3 17 F1
Latton Clo. SN2 9 G1
Lawrence Clo. SN3 17 F3
Lawton Clo. SN3 16 C6
Lea Clo. SN2 5 C4
Leamington Gro. SN3 16 C5
Leicester St. SN1 3 C3
Leigh Rd. SN2 9 H2
Leighton Av. SN3 16 D4
Lennox Dri. SN3 16 C2
Leslie Clo. SN5 14 B3
Lethbridge Rd. SN1 3 C6
Letterage Rd. SN5 8 B4
Leven. SN5 10 B5
Leverton Gate. SN3 16 C6
*Lewis Clo,
  Hepworth Rd. SN2 9 F1
Lewisham Clo. SN2 9 E4
Lichen Clo. SN2 8 D3
Liddington St. SN2 10 A4
Liden Dri. SN3 17 F4
Limes Av. SN3 9 G4
Lincoln St. SN1 3 C3
Linden Av. SN2 9 H4
Linden Way. SN5 8 B4
Lineacre Clo. SN5 14 A4
Link Av. SN5 14 C2
Linley Clo. SN3 16 A5
Linley Rd. SN2 5 E2
Linnetsdene. SN3 11 F6
Linslade St. SN2 15 F2
Lisle Clo. SN5 14 A3
Little Av. SN2 9 F5
Little London. SN1 3 C5
Littlecote Clo. SN5 6 C2
Locks La. SN5 6 C3
Locksgreen Cres. SN2 9 E3
Logan Clo. SN3 16 B2
Lomond Clo. SN5 8 C5
London St. SN1 3 A2
Long Acre. SN5 6 C3
Longfellow Clo. SN4 5 C3
Longstock Ct. SN5 14 D3
Longthorpe Clo. SN5 14 D3
Lonsdale Clo. SN2 5 E2

Lorne St. SN1 15 G2
Loughborough Clo. SN5 14 A3
Louviers Way. SN1 16 A5
Loveage Clo. SN2 8 D3
Loveridge Clo. SN2 10 B1
Lovell Clo. SN3 17 F1
Lowes Clo. SN5 8 C4
Lucerne Clo. SN5 14 A1
Luddesdown Rd. SN5 14 C4
Ludgershall Rd. SN5 15 E4
Ludlow Clo. SN3 16 C4
Lulworth Rd. SN2 9 E3
Lumley Clo. SN5 14 A3
Lutyens Gate. SN3 19 G1
Lyall Clo. SN2 5 B3
Lyddon Way. SN2 9 F3
Lydford Clo. SN5 8 B6
Lydiard Grn. SN5 7 B6
Lyme Way. SN2 9 F2
Lyndhurst Cres. SN3 16 D2
Lyneham Clo. SN3 9 H1
Lynton Rd. SN2 9 E5
Lynwood Gro. SN2 8 D3
Lytchett Way. SN3 17 F2

Mackenzie Clo. SN3 17 G4
Magpie La. SN3 17 G1
Maidstone Rd. SN1 3 A5
Maitland Rd. SN3 16 D1
Majestic Clo. SN5 14 A1
Maldwyn Clo. SN5 14 A1
Mallard Clo. SN3 17 G2
Mallow Clo. SN2 8 D2
Malthouse Clo. SN2 5 D1
Malvern Rd. SN2 9 H5
Manchester Rd. SN1 3 B2
Mannington Employment
  Area. SN5 15 E3
Mannington La. SN5 14 D3
Mannington Pk. SN2 15 E1
Manor Clo. SN2 5 E2
Manor Cres. SN2 9 E4
Manor Gdns. SN2 9 E4
Manor Pk. SN3 11 G3
Manor St. SN1 15 F3
Manor View. SN4 20 B5
Manton St. SN2 15 F1
Maple Gro. SN2 9 H4
March Clo. SN2 9 F1
Mardale Clo. SN5 8 A6
Margarets Grn. SN3 11 E4
Marigold Clo. SN3 8 D2
Marjoram Clo. SN2 8 D2
Markenfield. SN5 14 D3
Market St. SN1 3 A3
Markham Clo. SN3 16 C1
Marlborough La. SN3 16 B5
Marlborough Rd. SN4 20 C3
Marlborough Rd. SN3 3 D6
Marlborough St. SN1 15 F3
Marlowe Av. SN3 16 D1
Marney Rd. SN5 14 B2
Marshall Rd. SN5 8 B6
Marshfield Way. SN3 10 D5
Marshgate. SN1 10 C6
Marshgate Ind Est. SN1 10 C6
Marsland Rd. SN2 10 B4
Marston Av. SN2 10 A2
Martinfield. SN3 17 F1
Masefield Av. SN2 10 B4
Matley Moor. SN3 17 G5
Maxey Clo. SN3 16 D4
Maxwell St. SN1 15 G2
May Clo. SN2 9 H5
Mayfield Clo. SN3 17 E1
Mays La. SN4 20 B5
Mead Way. SN5 14 C1
Meadow La. SN4 20 D3
Meadow Rd. SN2 15 E1
Meadow Springs. SN5 7 E6
Meadow Way. SN4 20 D3
Meadowcroft. SN2 10 C2
Meadowsweet Clo. SN2 9 E1
Meares Dri. SN5 8 B6
Medbury Pl. SN1 3 C2
Medbury Rd. SN1 3 C2
Medina Way. SN2 10 C2
Medway Rd. SN2 9 F3
Melbourne Clo. SN3 16 D5
Medbourne La. SN4 20 D3
Melford Walk. SN3 17 E1
Melfort Clo. SN5 8 C5
Melksham Clo. SN2 9 G1
Mellow Ground. SN2 9 E3
Melrose Clo. SN5 14 C1
Melville Clo. SN3 16 C2

Melvyn Webb Pl. SN2 10 B6
Mendip Clo. SN2 9 H3
Menham Clo. SN2 10 A4
Merlin Way. SN3 11 F6
Merrivale Gro. SN3 16 B3
Merton Av. SN2 10 B3
Merton St. SN1 3 B2
Meynell Clo. SN2 5 B3
Middleleaze Dri. SN5 14 A1
Middleton Clo. SN3 16 C2
Midhurst Av. SN3 17 E2
Midwinter Clo. SN5 8 B5
Midwinter Gdns. SN3 10 D4
Mildenhall Way. SN2 9 G1
Mildmay Clo. SN5 14 A3
Miles Clo. SN2 10 C3
Milford St. SN1 3 B2
Mill La. SN1 15 F5
Millbuck Clo. SN2 10 C5
Miller Clo. SN5 14 A1
Milston Av. SN2 9 H2
Milton Rd. SN1 3 A3
Minety Rd. SN2 9 G1
Minster Clo. SN2 5 B4
Mint Clo. SN2 8 D3
Monet Clo. SN3 9 F1
Monkton Clo. SN3 17 E4
Monmouth Clo. SN3 16 C4
Montague St. SN2 15 E1
Monteagle Clo. SN5 14 A3
Montgomery Av. SN2 9 G5
Montrose Clo. SN3 9 E4
Moorhen Clo. SN3 16 G2
Mopes La. SN5 6 D1
Moray Rd. SN3 10 B5
Moredon Pk. SN2 8 D3
Moredon Rd. SN2 9 E3
Moresby Clo. SN5 14 C2
Morie Clo. SN5 8 C5
Morley St. SN1 3 B3
Morris St. SN2 15 E2
Morrison St. SN2 15 E1
Morse St. SN1 3 A4
Mortimer Clo. SN5 14 C1
Mud La. SN5 6 A4
Mulberry Gro. SN2 9 F4
Mulcaster Av. SN5 14 A3
Mundy Av. SN3 17 E3
Munro Clo. SN3 16 B2
Murdoch Rd. SN3 17 G2
Myrtle Gdns. SN2 9 H4

Nantwich. SN5 14 B5
Napier Clo. SN3 15 F1
Nash Clo. SN2 5 C3
Naunton Rd. SN3 16 D2
Nelson St. SN1 15 F3
Ness Clo. SN5 8 C4
Netherton Clo. SN3 17 E4
Nevis Clo. SN5 8 C4
New Bridge Clo. SN1 3 B2
New Bridge Sq. SN1 3 B2
New Meadow Copse.
  SN5 8 B5
New Rd. SN4 20 B5
New Rd. SN5 6 C1
Newark Clo. SN5 14 B4
Newburn Cres. SN1 15 F3
Newbury Dri. SN5 14 B4
Newcastle St. SN1 3 C3
Newcome Dri. SN2 15 F1
Newhall St. SN1 3 A4
Newland Rd. SN2 9 F3
Newport St. SN1 3 C6
*Newstead Clo,
  Bicton Rd. SN2 9 F1
Newton Way. SN2 9 H3
Nightingale Rd. SN3 11 H3
Nightwood Copse. SN5 8 B5
Nindum Rd. SN3 11 E5
Nolan Clo. SN2 5 B3
Norcliffe Rd. SN3 16 D4
Norfolk Clo. SN3 16 D2
Norman Rd. SN2 9 H6
Norris Clo. SN4 20 B6
North St. SN1 3 C5
North Star Av. SN2 3 A1
Northampton St. SN1 3 D3
Northbourne Rd. SN2 5 C4
Northbrook Rd. SN2 9 G5
Northern Rd. SN2 9 G6
Northfield Way. SN3 17 E1
Northleaze Clo. SN3 9 F4
Norton Gro. SN3 3 D4
Norwood Clo. SN3 17 F4
Nuffield Clo. SN5 14 C1

Nunwell Clo. SN2 5 C4
Nuthatch Clo. SN3 17 G2
Nutmeg Clo. SN2 8 D3
Nyland Rd. SN3 17 E1
Nythe Rd. SN3 11 E5

Oak Garden. SN3 10 D3
Oak Tree Av. SN2 10 A4
Oakford Walk. SN3 16 D2
Oakham Clo. SN5 14 C3
Oakie Clo. SN2 9 G1
Oaksey Rd. SN2 9 H2
Oakwood Rd. SN5 14 C1
Oasthouse Clo. SN5 8 A6
Oberon Way. SN2 9 F2
Ocotol Way. SN1 3 D1
Odstock Rd. SN2 9 H1
Okebourne Pk. SN3 17 F5
Okeford Clo. SN3 17 E1
Okus Gro. SN2 10 B3
Okus Ind Est. SN1 15 G4
Okus Rd. SN2 3 A6
Old Mill La. SN3 3 D6
Old Shaw La. SN5 14 B1
Old Vicarage La. SN3 11 H3
Olive Gro. SN2 9 G4
Oliver Clo. SN5 14 A2
Oliver Rd. SN2 5 D4
Omdurman St. SN2 9 H6
Orchard Gdns. SN5 6 B3
Orchard Gro. SN2 10 B3
Orchid Clo. SN2 9 H3
Oriel St. SN1 3 B2
Orkney Clo. SN5 14 B2
Orlando Clo. SN5 14 A3
Orrin Clo. SN5 8 C5
Orwell Clo. SN3 9 F2
Osborne St. SN2 9 G6
Osprey Clo. SN3 17 G2
Osterley Rd. SN2 9 E1
Overbrooke. SN3 17 E4
Overton Clo. SN3 11 E5
Owl Clo. SN3 16 G2
Oxford Rd. SN3 10 D5
Oxford St. SN1 3 A2

Packington Clo. SN5 14 B1
Paddington Dri. SN5 15 E2
Paddock Clo. SN2 9 E2
Pakenham Rd. SN3 17 E4
Parham Walk. SN5 14 A3
Park La. SN5 7 E6
Park La. SN1 15 F2
Park Side. SN3 10 D4
Park Springs. SN5 14 D3
Park St. SN3 11 E5
Park View Dri. SN5 7 E6
Parklands Rd. SN3 16 B3
Parr Clo. SN5 14 A2
Parsley Clo. SN2 8 D2
Parsonage Rd. SN3 10 D3
Partridge Clo. SN3 17 H2
Passmore Clo. SN3 17 G1
Pasture Clo. SN2 15 E1
Patney Walk. SN2 9 G1
Paulet Clo. SN5 14 A3
Paven Clo. SN5 6 B3
Pavenhill. SN5 6 A3
Peaks Down. SN5 8 B4
Pear Tree Clo. SN5 6 D2
Pearce Clo. SN2 10 C1
Pearl Rd. SN5 14 A1
Peatmoor Way. SN5 8 B5
Pembroke Gdns. SN2 9 F3
Pembroke St. SN1 3 B5
Pen Clo. SN3 9 G3
Pencarrow Clo. SN2 9 E1
Pendennis. SN5 14 B4
Penfold Gdns. SN1 3 B6
Penhill Dri. SN2 9 H1
Pennine Way. SN2 5 B4
Penny La. SN3 16 C1
Pennycress Clo. SN2 8 D3
Pentridge Clo. SN3 17 F1
Penzance Dri. SN5 14 B3
Pepperbox Hill. SN5 8 B5
Percheron Clo. SN5 14 B1
Percy St. SN2 15 F1
Peregrine Clo. SN3 11 F6
Periwinkle Clo. SN2 8 C3
Petersfield Rd. SN3 17 E4
Pevensey Way. SN3 14 C3
Pewsham Rd. SN2 10 A2
Pheasant Clo. SN3 17 G2
*Pickford Way,
  Hayward Clo. SN2 9 G1

Pickwick Clo. SN2 10 B2
Picton Rd. SN5 14 B1
Pigeon House La. SN3 10 D4
Pilgrim Clo. SN5 14 B1
Pilton Clo. SN5 8 A6
Pinehurst Rd. SN2 9 G5
Pinetree Rise. SN2 9 G4
Pinnegar Way. SN3 17 G2
Pinnocks Pl. SN2 10 C3
Pioneer Clo. SN5 14 A1
Pipers Way. SN3 16 A6
Pipitdene. SN3 17 G1
Plattes Clo. SN5 8 C6
Play Clo. SN5 6 D3
Pleydell Rd. SN1 16 A5
Plymouth St. SN1 3 C3
Poltondale. SN3 17 G1
Pond St. SN2 9 E2
Ponting St. SN1 3 C1
Poole Rd. SN2 9 E3
Pope Clo. SN2 9 E1
Poplar Av. SN2 9 H4
Popplechurch Dri. SN3 17 G1
Portal Rd. SN2 9 G5
Portland Av. SN1 15 G4
Portmore Clo. SN5 8 C5
Portsmouth St. SN1 3 D2
Potterdown Rd. SN2 9 H1
Poulton St. SN2 9 H6
Pound La. SN2 9 G4
Poynings Way. SN5 14 A3
Primrose Clo. SN2 8 D1
Princes St. SN1 3 C3
Priory Rd. SN3 16 D4
Pritchard Clo. SN2 10 C2
Prospect Hill. SN1 3 B4
Prospect Pl. SN1 3 C5
Proud Clo. SN5 6 C4
Purbeck Clo. SN3 17 E1
Purley Av. SN3 17 E5
Purley Rd. SN4 17 H6
Purslane Clo. SN5 8 C3
Purton Rd. SN2 8 D3

Quarry Brook Clo. SN3 11 G2
Quarry Mews. SN1 15 H4
Quarry Rd. SN1 3 B6
Queen St. SN1 3 A3
Queen Elizabeth Dri.
  SN2 8 C2
Queenborough. SN5 14 C4
Queens Dri. SN3 3 D2
Queensfield. SN2 10 B1
Quentin Rd. SN3 16 B4

Radcot Clo. SN5 8 B6
Radley Clo. SN3 17 E1
Radnor St. SN1 15 G3
Radstock Av. SN3 17 E2
Radway Rd. SN3 10 D4
Raggett St. SN1 3 B4
Raglan Clo. SN3 16 C5
Rainer Clo. SN3 11 E4
Raleigh Av. SN3 16 C2
Ramleaze Dri. SN5 14 B1
Ramsbury Av. SN2 9 G1
Ramsden Rd. SN5 14 A5
Ramsthorn Clo. SN2 8 D3
Randall Cres. SN5 14 B1
Randolph Clo. SN3 16 C2
Rannoch Clo. SN5 8 C5
Ratcombe Rd. SN3 8 B6
Ravenglass Rd. SN5 14 C2
Ravenscroft. SN3 17 F1
Rawlings Clo. SN3 11 G3
Rawston Clo. SN3 17 F2
Ray Clo. SN2 9 F2
Raybrook Cres. SN2 15 E2
Rayfield Gro. SN2 9 G6
Read St. SN1 15 G3
Reading St. SN1 3 A2
Redbridge Clo. SN5 15 E3
Redcap Gdns. SN5 14 B1
Redcliffe St. SN2 15 F2
Redlynch Clo. SN2 9 H1
Redposts Dri. SN5 15 E4
Redruth Clo. SN3 17 E3
Regent Circus. SN1 3 B4
Regent Clo. SN1 3 B3
Regent St. SN1 3 B3
Regents Pl. SN1 10 C6
Reids Piece. SN5 6 C3
*Renoir Clo,
  Wallis Dri. SN2 5 C3
Restrop Rd. SN5 6 B4

Restrop View. SN5 6 B3
Retingham Way. SN3 10 D2
Revell Clo. SN2 10 B2
Reynolds Way. SN5 2 C3
Rhine Clo. SN5 15 E4
Rhuddlan. SN5 14 C4
Richard Jefferies
　Gdns. SN4 20 C5
Richmond Rd. SN2 9 F6
Ridge Grn. SN5 14 C1
Ridge Nether Moor.
　SN3 17 G5
Ridgeway Clo. SN2 9 E4
Ridgeway Rd. SN2 10 B1
Ringsbury Clo. SN5 6 A3
Ringwood Clo. SN3 17 E2
Rinsdale Clo. SN5 8 C5
Ripley Rd. SN1 3 C6
Ripon Way. SN3 16 D4
Ripplefield. SN5 14 B4
Risingham Mead. SN5 14 C3
Rivenhall Rd. SN5 14 C2
Riverdale Clo. SN1 16 A6
Rivermead Dri. SN5 14 C1
Rivermead Ind Est. SN5 8 C6
Robins Grn. SN3 17 F1
Robinson Clo. SN3 17 F2
Roche Clo. SN3 17 F4
Rochester Clo. SN5 14 B4
Rochford Clo. SN5 14 A3
Rockdown Ct. SN2 9 H2
Rodbourne Grn. SN2 9 F5
Rodbourne Rd. SN2 9 F6
Rodwell Clo. SN3 16 D3
Rogers Clo. SN3 16 D1
Rolleston St. SN1 3 B4
Roman Cres. SN1 15 G5
Romney Way. SN5 14 B2
Romsey St. SN2 15 F1
Rose Dale Rd. SN3 16 D4
Rose St. SN2 15 E1
Rosebery St. SN1 3 C1
Rosemary Clo. SN2 8 D2
Ross Gdns. SN3 10 D2
Rother Clo. SN2 9 E2
Roughmoor Way. SN5 14 B1
Roundway Down. SN5 14 C5
Rowan Rd. SN2 9 F4
Rowland Hill Clo. SN3 17 G4
Rowton Heath Way.
　SN5 14 B3
Royston Rd. SN3 16 D4
Rubens Clo. SN2 5 B3
Ruckley Gdns. SN3 11 E5
Rushall Clo. SN2 9 G2
Rushton Rd. SN3 16 D4
Ruskin Av. SN2 10 C3
Russell Walk. SN3 16 C2
Russley Clo. SN5 8 A5
Ryan Clo. SN5 8 C4
Rycote Clo. SN5 14 B2
Rydal Clo. SN2 9 F2
Rye Clo. SN5 14 B1

Sackville Clo. SN3 16 C1
Saddleback Rd. SN5 14 B1
Sadler Walk. SN3 16 C3
Saffron Clo. SN3 8 D3
Sage Clo. SN3 8 D2
St Albans Clo. SN2 15 E1
St Ambrose Clo. SN3 17 G2
St Andrews Ct. SN2 5 B3
St Andrews Grn. SN3 17 G1
St Helens Vw. SN1 15 F4
St James Clo. SN2 10 B2
St Katherines Grn. SN3 17 G1
St Margarets Rd. SN3 16 A4
St Marys Gro. SN3 9 G6
St Pauls Dri. SN3 17 F1
St Pauls St. SN2 9 H6
St Philips Rd. SN2 10 B3
Salcombe Gro. SN3 16 C3
Salisbury St. SN1 3 C1
Salthrop Rd. SN4 13 H5
Saltram Clo. SN3 17 E2
Saltzgitter Dri. SN2 5 C3
Sams La. SN2 5 E2
Sandacre Rd. SN5 8 A6
*Sandford Ct,
　Springfield Rd. SN1 15 H4
Sandgate. SN3 11 E5
Sandown Av. SN3 16 B4
Sandpiper Bri. SN3 17 G1
Sandringham Rd. SN3 17 G1
Sandstone Rd. SN2 5 B4
Sandwood Clo. SN5 8 C5

Sandy La. SN1 3 A6
Sanford St. SN1 3 B3
Sarsen Clo. SN1 15 F4
Savernake St. SN1 3 B4
Saxon Mill. SN4 20 C4
　School Clo. SN4 20 C5
　School Row. SN3 9 E3
Scotby Av. SN3 16 B5
Scotney Cres. SN3 9 F1
Seaton Clo. SN2 9 F2
Sedgebrook. SN3 17 F5
Selby Cres. SN5 14 B3
Severn Av. SN2 9 F2
Seymour Rd. SN3 16 C2
Shaftesbury Av. SN5 17 E5
Shakespeare Path. SN2 10 C3
Shalbourne Clo. SN5 14 C1
Shanklin Rd. SN2 9 E3
Shaplands. SN3 10 D4
Shapwick Clo. SN5 17 F1
Sharp Clo. SN5 14 C1
Shaw Rd. SN5 14 C1
Shearwood Rd. SN5 8 B5
Sheen Clo. SN5 14 A4
Shelley St. SN1 3 A4
Shellfinch. SN5 14 D4
Shenton Clo. SN3 11 E4
Sheppard St. SN1 3 A2
Shepperton Way. SN2 9 F1
Sherbourne Pl. SN3 16 C2
Sherford Rd. SN2 9 E3
Sherston Av. SN2 9 H2
Sherwold Clo. SN3 11 E3
Sherwood Rd. SN3 17 E4
Shetland Clo. SN5 14 B1
Shipley Dri. SN2 9 E1
Shipton Gro. SN3 16 B3
Shire Clo. SN5 14 B1
Shire Ct. SN1 15 F3
Shirley Clo. SN3 16 C1
Shrewsbury Rd. SN3 16 C2
Shrewton Walk. SN2 9 H1
Shrivenham Rd. SN1 3 D2
Shropshire Clo. SN5 14 B1
Sidney Clo. SN3 14 A3
Signal Way. SN3 16 B4
Silchester Way. SN5 14 C2
Silto Ct. SN2 9 F5
Silverton Rd. SN3 17 E2
Simnel Clo. SN5 14 A3
Slade Dri. SN3 10 D6
Sleaford Clo. SN5 14 A2
Slipper La. SN4 20 B5
Smitan Brook. SN3 17 F2
Snowdrop Clo. SN2 8 D3
Snowshill Clo. SN2 9 F2
Somerdale Clo. SN5 14 C2
Somerford Clo. SN2 10 A3
Somerset Rd. SN2 9 F5
Somerville Rd. SN3 16 C2
Sound Copse. SN5 8 B4
South Marston Park
　Ind Est. SN3 11 F1
South St. SN1 3 C5
South View Av. SN3 16 B2
Southampton St. SN1 3 D3
Southbrook St. SN2 9 G6
Southernwood Dri. SN2 8 C2
Southey Clo. SN3 5 B3
Southwick Av. SN2 9 G2
Sparcells Dri. SN5 8 C4
Speedwell Clo. SN2 9 E1
Spencer Clo. SN5 14 A1
Spencer Clo. SN3 16 D1
Spersholt. SN5 14 D4
Spring Clo. SN1 3 C3
Spring Gdns. SN1 3 C3
Spring Hill Clo. SN5 14 C3
Springfield Rd. SN1 16 A4
Spur Way. SN3 10 C3
Squires Copse. SN5 8 B5
Stafford St. SN1 3 A4
Stamford Clo. SN5 14 C3
Stanbridge Pk. SN5 14 B1
Stancombe Pk. SN5 14 D3
Standen Way. SN2 5 C4
Standings Clo. SN5 8 A6
Stanier St. SN1 3 B4
Stanley St. SN1 3 C5
Stanmore St. SN1 15 G3
Stansfield Clo. SN5 14 D4
Stanway Clo. SN3 16 D3
Stapleford Clo. SN2 9 G1
Staring Clo. SN5 8 A6
Station App. SN1 3 C6

Station Rd. SN4 20 C5
Station Rd. SN5 6 D2
Station Rd. SN1 3 A2
*Staverton Way,
　Westwood Rd. SN2 9 H1
Stenbury Clo. SN2 5 C4
Stenness Clo. SN5 8 C4
Stephens Rd. SN3 10 D6
Stewart Clo. SN2 9 G1
Stirling Rd. SN3 11 F1
*Stockbridge Copse,
　Ratcombe Rd. SN5 8 B4
Stockton Rd. SN2 9 H2
Stokesay Dri. SN5 14 C3
Stone La. SN5 7 D5
Stonecrop Way. SN2 9 E1
Stonefield Clo. SN5 14 C1
Stonehill Grn. SN5 14 D2
Stonehurst Rd. SN3 10 D6
Stoneybeck Clo. SN5 14 D2
Stratford Clo. SN5 14 D3
Stratton Orchard. SN3 10 D4
Stratton Rd. SN1 10 C6
Stratton Rd Ind Est.
　SN2 10 C6
Stratton St Margaret
　By-Pass. SN2 10 B1
Strouds Hill. SN4 20 B5
Stuart Clo. SN3 16 D2
Stubsmead. SN3 17 F3
Studland Clo. SN3 17 E4
Sudeley Way. SN5 14 B3
Suffolk St. SN2 9 H6
Summers St. SN2 15 F1
Sunningdale Rd. SN2 9 H3
Sunnyside Av. SN1 15 F3
Surrey Rd. SN2 9 F5
Sutton Park. SN2 5 E2
Sutton Rd. SN3 17 F4
Swallowdale. SN3 17 F1
Swallowfield Av. SN3 16 C3
Swanbrook. SN3 11 F6
Swift Av. SN2 5 C4
Swindon Rd. SN3 10 D6
Swindon Rd. SN1 3 B5
Swinley Dri. SN5 8 A5
Sword Gdns. SN5 15 F4
Sycamore Gro. SN3 9 H4
Symonds. SN5 14 B5
Syon Clo. SN2 9 F1
Sywell Rd. SN3 11 F6

Tamar Clo. SN2 9 G3
Tamworth Dri. SN5 14 B2
Tansley Moor. SN3 17 G5
*Tarka Clo,
　W. Highland Rd. SN2 5 B4
Tarragon Clo. SN2 8 C3
Tattershall. SN5 14 C4
Taunton St. SN1 15 G2
Tavistock Rd. SN3 17 E2
Tawny Owl Clo. SN3 11 E6
Taylor Cres. SN3 10 D2
Tealsbrook. SN3 17 G1
Techno Trading Est.
　SN2 10 C5
Tedder Clo. SN2 9 G5
Tees Clo. SN2 9 F2
Teeswater Clo. SN5 14 B2
Telford Way. SN5 14 D3
Temple St. SN1 3 B3
Tenby Clo. SN3 16 C4
Tennyson St. SN1 3 A3
Tensing Gdns. SN2 9 H3
Terncliff. SN3 17 F2
Tewkesbury Way. SN5 14 A1
Thackeray Clo. SN3 17 F4
Thames Av. SN2 9 E2
Thamesdown Dri,
　Abbey Meads. SN2 5 C4
Thamesdown Dri,
　Haydon. SN2 8 C3
The Acorns. SN3 16 D5
The Beeches. SN5 7 C5
The Birches. SN5 16 D5
The Bramptons. SN5 14 C1
The Brow. SN3 9 E2
The Bungalows. SN3 7 D6
The Buntings. SN3 17 F1
The Butts. SN5 7 D6
The Canney. SN4 20 C5
The Chesters. SN3 14 D2
The Circle. SN3 9 H4
The Close. SN3 7 D6
The Close. SN5 11 E4

The Common. SN5 6 C2
The Copse. SN2 5 D2
The Crescent. SN3 8 A4
The Crescent. SN4 20 B6
The Curnicks. SN3 20 B5
The Drive. SN3 17 E1
The Ferns. SN2 9 H6
The Forum. SN3 14 C3
The Fox. SN5 6 F4
The Harriers. SN3 17 F1
The Heights. SN1 15 F4
The Holbein. SN5 14 B3
The Hyde. SN5 6 D3
The Knoll. SN1 16 A5
The Mall. SN1 3 A5
The Marsh. SN4 17 H5
The Meadows. SN4 7 A8
The Masons. SN5 6 B3
The Mews. SN5 7 E6
The Orchard. SN4 20 C5
The Orchards. SN3 16 C6
The Owletts. SN3 17 G1
The Paddocks. SN3 10 D5
The Paddocks. SN5 7 E6
The Parade. SN1 3 B3
The Peak. SN5 6 C3
The Planks. SN3 3 D6
The Quarries. SN1 15 H4
The Ridge. SN2 5 D2
The Ridgeway. SN4 20 C6
The Square. SN1 3 D6
The Street. SN5 7 D6
The Street. SN3 9 E3
The Weavers. SN3 3 D6
The Willows. SN5 8 A4
Theatre Sq. SN1 3 B3
Theobald St. SN1 15 G2
Thetford Way. SN2 8 C2
Thirlmere. SN3 17 G4
Thomas St. SN2 15 F1
Thornbridge Av. SN3 16 D4
Thorne Rd. SN3 17 F4
Thornford Dri. SN5 14 C2
Thornhill Dri. SN2 5 B3
Thornhill Ind Est. SN3 11 G3
Thornhill Rd. SN3 11 G4
Thrushel Clo. SN2 9 E3
Thurlestone Rd. SN3 16 D4
Thurney Dri. SN5 14 A3
Thyme Clo. SN2 8 C3
Tidworth Clo. SN5 15 E4
Tilleys La. SN3 10 D5
Tilshead Walk. SN2 9 H2
Timandra Clo. SN2 9 H2
Tintagel Clo. SN5 14 C4
Tisbury Clo. SN2 9 H1
Tismeads Cres. SN1 16 A5
Titchfield Clo. SN5 14 A3
Tithe Barn Cres. SN1 15 F4
Tiverton Rd. SN2 9 H5
Tockenham Way. SN2 9 G1
Tollard Clo. SN3 17 F2
Torridge Clo. SN2 9 E3
Totterdown Clo. SN3 17 G1
Tovey Rd. SN2 9 G5
Tower Rd. SN5 8 B5
Tracy Clo. SN2 9 F1
Trajan Rd. SN3 11 F6
Transfer Bridge Ind Est.
　SN1 10 B6
Tree Courts Rd. SN2 9 H4
Tregantle Walk. SN3 17 E2
Tregoze Way. SN5 14 A2
Trent Rd. SN2 9 F3
Trentham Clo. SN3 16 D4
Trinity Clo. SN3 16 D4
Trueman Clo. SN3 17 F3
Truro Path. SN5 14 C3
Tryon Clo. SN3 17 G5
Tudor Cres. SN3 11 E5
Tulip Tree Clo. SN2 9 H4
Turl St. SN1 3 B2
Turnball. SN4 20 B5
Turner St. SN1 15 F3
Turnham Grn. SN5 14 B4
Turnpike Rd. SN6 5 D3
Tweed Clo. SN2 9 E2
Twyford Clo. SN3 16 D4
Tyburn Clo. SN5 14 B2
Tydeman St. SN2 10 A5
Tye Gdns. SN5 14 A3
Tyndale Path. SN5 14 A2
Tyneham Rd. SN3 17 E2

Ullswater Clo. SN3 17 G4

Union Row. SN1 3 C
Union St. SN1 3 C
Upfield. SN3 17 G
Upham Rd. SN3 3 D
Upper Pavenhill. SN5 6 A
Utah Clo. SN5 15 E
Uxbridge Rd. SN5 14 A

Valleyside. SN1 15 F
Vanbrugh Gate. SN3 16 D
Vasterne Clo. SN5 6 C
Ventnor Clo. SN2 9 E
Verney Clo. SN3 17 G
Verulam Clo. SN3 11 F
Verwood Clo. SN3 16 D
Vespasian Clo. SN3 11 F
Vicarage Rd. SN2 9 F
Victoria Rd. SN2 3 C
Viking Clo. SN2 5 B
Vilett St. SN1 3 A
Villiers Clo. SN5 14 A
Viscount Way. SN3 11 F
Volpe Clo. SN5 14 A
Volta Rd. SN1 3 C

Wagtail Clo. SN3 11 E6
Wainwright Clo. SN3 17 F3
Waite Meads Clo. SN5 6 D2
Wakefield Clo. SN5 14 B3
Walcot Rd. SN3 3 D4
Wallingford Clo. SN5 14 C4
Wallis Dri. SN2 5 C3
Wallsworth Rd. SN3 16 D3
Walnut Tree Gdns. SN5 7 E6
Walsingham Rd. SN3 16 C2
Walter Clo. SN5 14 B2
Walton Clo. SN3 16 D4
Walwayne Field. SN3 10 D2
Wanborough Rd,
　Covingham. SN3 17 G1
Wanborough Rd,
　Lower Stratton. SN3 11 F5
Warbeck Gate. SN5 14 A3
Wardley Clo. SN3 16 D4
Wardour Clo. SN3 16 C5
Wareham Clo. SN5 14 B3
Warminster Av. SN2 9 H1
Warneford Clo. SN5 14 D4
Warner Clo. SN3 11 E3
Warwick Rd. SN1 3 B4
Water Field. SN5 6 B3
Watercrook Mews. SN5 14 D3
Waterdown Clo. SN3 8 C2
Watermead. SN3 11 F4
Watling Clo. SN2 15 E2
Wavell Rd. SN2 9 G4
Waverley Rd. SN3 11 E6
Wayne Clo. SN2 9 F2
Wayside Clo. SN3 15 E1
Webbs Wood. SN5 8 B4
Wedgewood Clo. SN2 15 F1
Weedon Rd. SN3 11 E6
Welcombe Av. SN3 16 D3
Welford Clo. SN3 11 E6
Well Clo. SN4 20 B5
Wellington St. SN1 3 B2
Wells St. SN1 3 C3
Welton Rd. SN5 14 D2
Wembley St. SN2 9 F6
Wensleydale Clo. SN5 14 B2
Wentworth Park. SN5 14 B3
Wesley St. SN1 3 C5
West End Rd. SN3 10 D5
West Highland Rd. SN2 5 B4
West Hill. SN3 5 D1
Westbrook Rd. SN3 9 G5
Westbury Rd. SN3 9 H2
Westcott Pl. SN1 15 F3
Westcott St. SN1 15 F3
Western St. SN1 3 C4
Westfield Way. SN3 8 D3
Westlea Dri. SN5 14 C2
Westlecot Rd. SN1 15 G5
Westmead Dri. SN5 14 D1
Westmead Ind Est. SN5 14 D1
Westminster Rd. SN5 14 C3
Westmorland Rd. SN1 3 D4
Westview Walk. SN3 17 E1
Westwood Rd. SN3 9 H1
Wey Clo. SN5 9 G2
Weyhill Clo. SN3 16 D3
Wheatlands. SN2 9 E3
Wheatstone Rd. SN3 17 G3
Wheeler Av. SN3 17 G1
Whilestone Way. SN3 11 E5
Whitbourne Av. SN3 16 C3

hitbread Clo. SN5 14 B1
hitby Gro. SN2 9 F6
hite Castle. SN5 14 C4
hite Edge Moor. SN3 17 G5
hitefield Cres. SN5 8 A5
hitehead St. SN1 3 A4
hitehill Way. SN5 14 A4
hitehouse Rd. SN2 9 H6
hitelands Rd. SN3 10 D6
hiteman St. SN2 9 H6
hitgift Clo. SN5 14 A2
hitmore Clo. SN2 14 A2
hitney St. SN1 3 B4
hittington Rd. SN5 14 C2
hitworth Rd. SN2 9 F4
hichelstok Clo. SN1 15 H5
 hick La. SN3 17 G6
hickdown Av. SN5 9 E4
hicks Clo. SN2 9 E2
hidham. SN5 6 D2
hidhill La. SN2 5 C2
higmore Av. SN3 16 C4
hilcot Av. SN2 10 A2
hilcox Clo. SN2 9 H4
hildern Sq. SN3 10 D3
hilkins Clo. SN2 10 C2
hilliam St. SN1 15 G3
hillis Way. SN5 6 C3
hillowbrook. SN5 6 D3
hillowherb Clo. SN2 9 E3
hillows Av. SN2 10 A3
hills Av. SN1 10 C6
hilmot Clo. SN5 14 A2
hilson Rd. SN2 9 F1
hilton Walk. SN2 9 H1
hiltshire Av. SN2 9 G6
himpole Clo. SN5 16 D4
hinchcombe Clo. SN5 14 A2
hinchester Clo. SN3 11 E5
hindbrook Mdw. SN3 10 D5
hindermere. SN3 17 G4
hindflower Rd. SN2 9 E1
hindmill Hill
  Business Pk. SN5 14 A5
hindmill Piece. SN4 20 C5
hindrush Rd. SN2 9 F3
hindsor Clo. SN4 7 A8
hindsor Rd. SN5 16 C5
hingfield. SN3 10 D2
hingfield Av. SN2 9 H1
hinifred St. SN3 16 B4
hinlaw Clo. SN5 14 C1
hinsley Clo. SN2 9 H2
hinstanley Clo. SN5 14 B4
hinterslow Rd. SN2 9 G2
hinwick Rd. SN5 14 B4
hirral Clo. SN2 5 B4
hiseman Clo. SN3 17 G2
hitfield Clo. SN5 6 C2
hitham Way. SN2 10 C2
hitts La. SN5 6 C2
hoburn Clo. SN2 9 F1
holsely Av. SN3 16 D4
hood Hall Dri. SN2 8 D3
hood St. SN1 16 A4
hoodbine Ter. SN3 17 F5
hoodbury Clo. SN5 8 A6
hoodchester. SN5 14 C2
hoodford Clo. SN2 9 H1
hoodside Av. SN3 16 C3
*Woodspring Ct,
  Grovelands Av. SN11 15 H5
hoodstock Rd. SN3 11 E6
hoollaton Clo. SN5 14 B3
hootton Bassett Rd.
  SN1 15 E3
hordsworth Dri. SN2 10 C3
horlidge Dri. SN5 14 C1
horsley Rd. SN5 14 A4
hrenswood. SN3 17 F1
*Wright Clo,
  Wallis Dri. SN2 5 C3
hwylye Clo. SN2 9 E3
hyndham Rd. SN5 15 F1
hynndale Clo. SN5 10 D2
hwyvern Clo. SN1 16 A5

hardley Clo. SN2 9 E4
harmouth Clo. SN5 14 B3
harnton Clo. SN5 8 B6
harrow Clo. SN2 8 D3
heats Clo. SN2 5 C3
*Yellowhammer Clo,
  Wagtail Clo. SN3 11 F6
heoman Clo. SN5 14 A1
heovil Clo. SN3 17 E3

Yew Tree Gdns. SN3 11 G3
Yiewsley Cres. SN3 11 E5
York Rd. SN1 3 C4

CALNE

Abberd La. SN11 21 D2
Abberd Way. SN11 21 C3
Alma Ter. SN11 21 B2
Anchor Rd. SN11 21 C3
Angell Clo. SN11 21 A3
Avebury Clo. SN11 21 A3
Azalea Clo. SN11 21 C5
Back Rd. SN11 21 C4
Baily Ho. SN11 21 C6
Bay Clo. SN11 21 C6
Baydon Gro. SN11 21 B1
Bentley Clo. SN11 21 C4
Beversbrook Rd. SN11 21 B1
Bishop Rd. SN11 21 B2
Blake Rd. SN11 21 C3
Bluebell Gro. SN11 21 C1
Bodinrar Ho. SN11 21 C3
Braemor Rd. SN11 21 A2
Bremhill Vw. SN11 21 A1
Brewers La. SN11 21 C4
Broken Cross. SN11 21 C4
Bryans Close Rd. SN11 21 B2
Campion Clo. SN11 21 B1
Calne Township Dri.
  SN11 21 B4
Canal Clo. SN11 21 B4
Carnegie Mews. SN11 21 B3
Carnegie Rd. SN11 21 C1
Carpenters Clo. SN11 21 A2
Castle St. SN11 21 B3
Castle Walk. SN11 21 A3
Castlefields. SN11 21 B3
Charlieu Av. SN11 21 C6
Chavey Well Ct. SN11 21 B1
Cherry Tree Ct. SN11 21 B1
Chilvester Hill. SN11 21 A3
Church St. SN11 21 B3
Churchill Clo. SN11 21 C4
Clark Av. SN11 21 C1
Colemans Clo. SN11 21 C3
Cop Croft. SN11 21 B3
Corfe Cres. SN11 21 A2
Cornflower Clo. SN11 21 C1
Cotswold Clo. SN11 21 D4
Coulter Ho. SN11 21 C3
Cowslip Gro. SN11 21 B1
Coxs Hill. SN11 21 B3
Curzon Clo. SN11 21 A3
Curzon St. SN11 21 A3
Dixon Way. SN11 21 B2
Downland Rd. SN11 21 B3
Druids Clo. SN11 21 A3
Duncan St. SN11 21 C1
Dunnet Clo. SN11 21 C2
Ebor Paddock. SN11 21 D6
Elm Clo. SN11 21 C6
Eningen Vw. SN11 21 B4
Ernle Rd. SN11 21 C2
Fairway. SN11 21 C6
Falcon Rd. SN11 21 D3
Fitzmaurice Sq. SN11 21 C3
Foreman St. SN11 21 C3
Foxglove Way. SN11 21 B1
Fynamore Gdns. SN11 21 B4
Fynamore Pl. SN11 21 C2
George Clo. SN11 21 C3
Grierson Clo. SN11 21 C3
Guthrie Clo. SN11 21 C1
Harris Rd. SN11 21 C1
Hazel Gro. SN11 21 B5
Hazell Clo. SN11 21 C3
Heather Way. SN11 21 C5
Heron Clo. SN11 21 D3
High St. SN11 21 B3
Highgrove Clo. SN11 21 D3
Holly Clo. SN11 21 C5
Honey Garston. SN11 21 C2
Honeymead. SN11 21 C2
Horsebrook. SN11 21 C4
Horsebrook Pk. SN11 21 C4
Hungerford Rd. SN11 21 C2
INDUSTRIAL ESTATES:
  Portemarsh Ind Est.
    SN11 21 C1
  Station Rd Ind Est.
    SN11 21 B4
Jasmine Clo. SN11 21 C5
Keevil Av. SN11 21 A3

Kerry Cres. SN11 21 B3
Kingsbury St. SN11 21 B3
Lansdowne Clo. SN11 21 A2
Lickhill Rd. SN11 21 B1
Lilac Way. SN11 21 B5
Lime Tree Clo. SN11 21 A3
Linden Clo. SN11 21 B4
*Lodge Clo, Longbarrow Rd.
  SN11 21 A3
London Rd. SN11 21 C4
Longbarrow Rd. SN11 21 A3
Low La. SN11 21 C4
Luckett Way. SN11 21 C1
Macaulay Sq. SN11 21 C1
Magnolia Rise. SN11 21 B5
Mallard Clo. SN11 21 D3
Maple Clo. SN11 21 C5
Marden Way. SN11 21 A3
Market Hill. SN11 21 B3
Martin Way. SN11 21 D3
Maundrell Rd. SN11 21 C1
Meadow Vw. SN11 21 D6
Mill St. SN11 21 B3
Nesleton Clo. SN11 21 B4
New Rd. SN11 21 B3
Newcroft Clo. SN11 21 C1
Newcroft Rd. SN11 21 B1
North End. SN11 21 A2
North St. SN11 21 B2
Northcote. SN11 21 A2
Northway. SN11 21 A2
Ogilvie Sq. SN11 21 C3
Oldbury Prior. SN11 21 C5
Oldbury Way. SN11 21 A3
Orchard Clo. SN11 21 C4
Oxford Rd. SN11 21 B3
Page Clo. SN11 21 C4
Park Clo. SN11 21 C4
Patford St. SN11 21 B3
Penn Hill Rd. SN11 21 C2
Phelps Par. SN11 21 B4
Pinhills. SN11 21 B4
Pinniger Ho. SN11 21 B4
Porte Marsh Rd. SN11 21 C1
Portland Pl. SN11 21 D4
Portland Way. SN11 21 D4
Priestley Gro. SN11 21 C4
Primrose Clo. SN11 21 B1
Prince Charles Dri.
  SN11 21 C3
Purbeck Clo. SN11 21 D4
Pym Ho. SN11 21 C3
Quarr Barton. SN11 21 B3
Quarrydale Clo. SN11 21 B1
Ridgemead. SN11 21 B1
Riverside. SN11 21 D6
Rochdale Av. SN11 21 B1
Roundhouse. SN11 21 D5
Saddle Back Clo. SN11 21 C4
Saffron Mdw. SN11 21 A3
St Catherines Clo. SN11 21 C2
St Dunstan Clo. SN11 21 B1
St Margarets Clo. SN11 21 A2
St Nicholas Clo. SN11 21 C2
Sand Pit Rd. SN11 21 D1
Sandy Ridge. SN11 21 B4
Sarum Way. SN11 21 A3
Savernake Dri. SN11 21 A3
Shelburne Rd. SN11 21 C4
Silbury Rd. SN11 21 A3
Silver St. SN11 21 B5
South Pl. SN11 21 B4
Springfield Dri. SN11 21 A2
Station Rd. SN11 21 B4
Stockley La. SN11 21 C6
Stokes Croft. SN11 21 B1
Swaddon St. SN11 21 B2
Tamarisk Clo. SN11 21 A5
Tern Clo. SN11 21 D3
The Glebe. SN11 21 C3
The Green. SN11 21 C4
The Knapp. SN11 21 C3
The Pippin. SN11 21 B3
The Quarry. SN11 21 B5
The Rise. SN11 21 C6
The Slades. SN11 21 B5
The Square. SN11 21 B3
The Strand. SN11 21 B3
The Wharf. SN11 21 B3
The Wynd. SN11 21 B2
Thomas Ct. SN11 21 C4
Trinity Pl. SN11 21 B5
Tyning Pk. SN11 21 C5
Valley View. SN11 21 B4
Vicarage Clo. SN11 21 C3
Victoria Ter. SN11 21 B2

*Walter Sutton Clo,
  Longbarrow Rd. SN11 21 A3
Wansdyke Dri. SN11 21 A3
Warren Cres. SN11 21 C2
Wenhill Heights. SN11 21 B4
Wenhill La. SN11 21 A4
Wessex Clo. SN11 21 D3
Wessington Av. SN11 21 C5
Wessington Ct. SN11 21 C5
Wessington Pk. SN11 21 D5
Westerhan Wk. SN11 21 D4
White Horse Way.
  SN11 21 B5
William St. SN11 21 C1
Winter Grn. SN11 21 A2
Wood St. SN11 21 B3
Woodhill Av. SN11 21 C2
Woodhill Rise. SN11 21 C2
Woodland Pk. SN11 21 B4
Woodroffe Sq. SN11 21 C3
Wyvern Av. SN11 21 D3
Yew Tree Clo. SN11 21 A3

CHIPPENHAM

Acacia Clo. SN14 22 A2
Allington Way. SN14 22 A2
Andrews Clo. SN14 22 B4
Applewood Clo. SN14 22 C3
Arundel Clo. SN14 22 A4
Ascot Clo. SN14 22 A6
Ashe Cres. SN15 22 D1
Ashfield Rd. SN15 22 D2
Audley Rd. SN14 22 C4
Avebury Rd. SN14 22 A5
Avenue La Fleche.
  SN15 22 D4
Avonmead. SN15 23 F3
Awdry Clo. SN14 22 A4
Bakehouse Clo. SN15 23 E4
Barken Rd. SN14 22 A2
Barn Clo. SN14 22 A3
Barn Owl Rd. SN14 22 B1
Barnes Rd. SN14 22 B1
Barons Mead. SN14 22 A3
Barrow Grn. SN15 23 E1
Bath Rd. SN14 22 A6
Bath Rd. SN15 22 C5
Baydons La. SN15 23 E5
Bayliffes Clo. SN15 23 G4
Beale Clo. SN14 22 A4
Beaver Mead. SN15 23 F6
Beechwood Rd. SN14 22 C3
Bellinger Clo. SN15 22 D1
Berkeley Clo. SN14 22 A4
Birch Gro. SN15 22 D2
Birds Marsh View.
  SN15 23 E1
Blackberry Clo. SN14 22 A1
Blackbridge Rd. SN15 23 F3
Blackcross. SN15 23 F5
Bluebell Dri. SN14 22 B1
Boothmead. SN14 22 B3
Borough Par. SN15 22 D4
Boundary Rd. SN15 23 F3
Bradbury Clo. SN15 23 G6
Brake Mead. SN15 23 F4
Bright Clo. SN15 23 F6
Brinkworth Clo. SN14 22 A5
Bristol Rd. SN15 22 A1
Brittain Clo. SN14 22 A4
Brook St. SN14 22 B3
Brookwell Clo. SN15 22 C1
Broomfield. SN15 22 D1
Brotherton Clo. SN15 23 F6
Bruges Clo. SN15 23 F4
Brunel Ct. SN15 22 B5
Bulls Hill. SN15 23 E5
Bumpers Way. SN14 22 A3
Bumpers Farm Way.
  SN14 22 A3
Burlands Rd. SN15 23 E5
Burleaze. SN15 22 C6
Bythebrook. SN14 22 B2
Canterbury St. SN14 22 A5
Carnarvon Clo. SN14 22 A5
Carpenter Clo. SN15 23 F6
Castlehaven Clo. SN15 23 G6
Causeway. SN15 23 E4
Causeway Clo. SN15 23 E4
Cedar Gro. SN15 23 E2
Celandine Way. SN14 22 B1
Chamberlain Rd. SN14 22 A2
Chapel La. SN15 23 E4

Charter Rd. SN15 22 D4
Cheltenham Dri. SN14 22 A6
Chelwood Clo. SN14 22 B5
Chepstow Clo. SN14 22 A6
Chester Way. SN14 22 A6
Chestnut Rd. SN14 22 C3
Chevral Clo. SN14 22 B1
Church View. SN15 22 C1
Clift Av. SN15 23 E2
Clift Ho. SN15 22 D2
Clifton Clo. SN14 22 B3
Clover Dean. SN14 22 A5
Cocklebury La. SN15 23 E1
Cocklebury Rd. SN15 23 E3
Colborne Clo. SN15 23 H6
College Clo. SN15 23 F3
Collen Clo. SN14 22 A4
Common Slip. SN15 23 E4
Coniston Rd. SN14 22 A4
Conway Rd. SN14 22 A4
Cranwell Clo. SN14 22 A6
Cricketts La. SN15 23 F6
Crown Clo. SN15 23 G6
Culverwell Rd. SN14 22 A4
Curlew Dri. SN14 22 A1
Dallas Rd. SN15 22 C3
Danes Clo. SN15 23 F6
Darcy Clo. SN15 23 F3
Deansway. SN15 22 D1
Deansway Ct. SN15 22 D1
Derby Clo. SN15 23 F6
Derriads Grn. SN14 22 A4
Derriads La. SN14 22 A4
Dover St. SN14 22 C4
Down View. SN14 22 A4
Downham Mead. SN15 23 F3
Downing St. SN14 22 C3
Dummer Way. SN15 23 G6
Dyers Clo. SN15 23 G6
Eastern Av. SN15 23 F3
Easton La. SN15 22 A6
Edridge Clo. SN15 23 F3
Elmwood. SN15 23 E1
Emery La. SN14 23 E4
Erleigh Dri. SN15 22 C4
Esmead. SN15 23 F3
Evans Clo. SN15 23 E2
Fairfoot Clo. SN14 22 A5
Fallowfield Clo. SN14 22 D1
Farleigh Clo. SN14 22 A5
Farmer Clo. SN15 23 E1
Field Vw. SN15 22 D4
Fleet Rd. SN15 22 D3
Foghamshire. SN15 22 D4
Folkestone Clo. SN14 22 A6
Forest La. SN15 23 F6
Fortune Way. SN15 23 F6
Foundry La. SN15 23 E3
Foxgrove. SN14 22 A1
Frogwell. SN14 22 A3
Frogwell Pk. SN14 22 A3
Gales Clo. SN15 23 F3
Garrick Clo. SN15 23 G3
Garth Clo. SN14 22 B1
Gascelyn Clo. SN14 22 A4
Gastons Rd. SN14 22 C3
Gipsy La. SN15 22 D5
Gladstone Rd. SN15 22 D4
Glendale Dri. SN15 23 E5
Gleneagles Clo. SN15 23 F4
Gloucester Clo. SN14 22 A5
Goldney Av. SN15 22 C4
Goodwood Way. SN14 22 A6
Greenway Av. SN15 22 D2
Greenway Ct. SN15 22 D1
Greenway Gdns. SN15 22 D2
Greenway La. SN15 22 D1
Greenway Pk. SN15 22 D2
Gundry Clo. SN15 23 F6
Habrels Clo. SN15 23 F5
Hancock Clo. SN14 23 G6
Hardenhuish Av. SN15 22 C3
Hardenhuish La. SN15 22 B2
Hardens Clo. SN15 23 E3
Hardens Mead. SN15 23 F3
Hares Patch. SN14 22 B1
Harford Clo. SN15 23 F6
Harnish Way. SN14 22 A5
Hawkins Clo. SN15 23 F6
Hawthorn Rd. SN15 23 E2
Haydock Clo. SN14 22 A6
Heathfield. SN15 23 E1
Hereford Clo. SN14 22 A6
Hewlett Clo. SN15 23 F6
High St. SN15 23 E4
Hill Corner Rd. SN15 22 D1

31

Hill Rise. SN15 22 D1
Hither Clo. SN14 22 D3
Hollybush Clo. SN14 22 A1
Honeybrook Clo. SN14 22 A3
Hungerdown La. SN14 22 A5
Hungerford Rd. SN15 22 D2
Huntingdon Way. SN14 22 A6
INDUSTRIAL ESTATES:
Bath Rd Ind Est. SN14 22 B5
Bumpers Farm
  Ind Est. SN14 22 A2
Greenways Business
  Park. SN15 22 D1
Herman Miller
  Ind Est. SN14 22 B6
Lansdowne Court
  Business Pk. SN14 22 A3
Parsonage Way
  Ind Est. SN15 23 F1
Ivy Field Ct. SN15 22 D4
Ivy La. SN15 22 D4
Ivy Rd. SN15 22 D4
Jasmine Clo. SN14 22 A2
Jordan Clo. SN15 23 F6
Kelso Ct. SN14 22 A6
Kent Clo. SN14 22 A5
Kilverts Clo. SN14 22 A5
King Alfred St. SN15 22 C3
Kingham Clo. SN14 22 C4
Kingsley Rd. SN14 22 B5
Lackham Circus. SN14 22 B5
Ladds La. SN15 23 E5
Lady Coventry Rd.
  SN15 23 F4
Ladyfield Rd. SN14 22 C2
Laines Head. SN15 22 C1
Lamberts. SN14 22 B3
Langley Rd. SN15 23 E2
Lanhill Vw. SN14 22 B1
Lansdown Gro. SN15 23 E2
Lapwing Cres. SN14 22 B1
Larkham Rise. SN15 23 F5
Laurel Dri. SN14 22 C5
Lenton Clo. SN14 22 A4
Little Down. SN14 22 B4
Little Englands. SN15 23 E5
Littlecote Rd. SN14 22 A5
Lockside. SN15 23 F6
Lodge Rd. SN15 23 G6
London Rd. SN15 23 F5
Long Clo. SN15 23 F5
Long Ridings. SN15 22 C1
Longstone. SN14 22 A2
Lords Mead. SN14 22 A3
Lovers Walk. SN15 22 D4
Lowden. SN14 22 C5
Lowden Av. SN15 22 C3
Lowden Hill. SN15 22 C4
Loyalty St. SN14 22 C4
Ludlow Clo. SN14 23 G6
Lydiard Rd. SN14 22 A5
Lytham Clo. SN14 23 F4
Malmesbury Rd. SN15 22 C1
Manor Rd. SN14 22 A3
Maple Way. SN15 22 D1
Market Pl. SN15 23 E4
Marlborough Ct. SN14 22 C4
Marshall St. SN14 22 C4
Marshfield Rd. SN15 22 C3
Martins Clo. SN15 23 G3
Matford Hill. SN15 23 G3
Maud Heaths
  Causeway. SN15 23 E1
Maur Clo. SN15 22 C4
Meadow Clo. SN14 22 A4
Melksham Rd. SN15 22 B6
Milestone Way. SN15 22 D1
Minster Way. SN14 22 A6
Monkton Hill. SN15 22 D4
Montague Clo. SN15 23 G4
Moorlands. SN15 23 E1
Mulberry Clo. SN14 22 B2
Murrayfield. SN15 23 E2
Neeld Cres. SN14 22 B3
New La. SN15 22 D3
New Rd. SN15 22 D3
Newall Tuck Rd. SN14 23 F4
Newbury Dri. SN14 22 A6
Northwood. SN15 23 E1
O'Donnell Clo. SN15 23 E1
Oak Lodge Clo. SN15 23 G3
Oaklands. SN15 22 D1
Oate Hill. SN15 23 F5
Odcroft Clo. SN15 23 F4
Old Hardenhuish La.
  SN14 22 B2

Old Rd. SN15 22 D3
Orchard Cres. SN14 22 B4
Orchard Rd. SN14 22 B4
Page Clo. SN14 22 A4
Palmer St. SN14 22 C4
Park Av. SN14 22 B3
Park La. SN15 22 D3
Park Ter. SN15 22 C3
Parkfields SN15 22 C3
Parkside. SN14 22 C3
Parliament St. SN14 22 B4
Parsonage Way. SN15 23 F1
Partridge Clo. SN14 22 B1
Patchway. SN14 22 B3
Pavely Clo. SN15 22 C5
Pew Hill. SN15 23 E1
Pewsham Lock. SN15 23 E6
Pewsham Way. SN15 23 E6
Picketleaze. SN14 22 A4
Pipsmore Rd. SN14 22 A3
Plantation. SN14 22 C3
Popham Ct. SN15 23 E5
Portway. SN14 22 B5
Primrose Way. SN14 22 B1
Queens Cres. SN14 22 A5
Queens Sq. SN15 23 E5
Ray Clo. SN15 23 F6
Redland. SN14 22 B3
Redwing Av. SN14 22 B1
Ricardo Rd. SN15 22 D3
Ridings Mead. SN15 22 C1
Ripon Clo. SN14 22 A6
River St. SN15 23 E4
Riverside Dri. SN15 23 F4
Robins Clo. SN14 22 B1
Roman Way. SN15 23 G6
Rowden Hill. SN15 22 C5
Rowden La. SN15 22 C6
Rowden Rd. SN15 22 C6
Rowe Mead. SN15 23 E6
Royal Clo. SN15 22 D5
Rumble Dene. SN15 23 E6
Ryan Av. SN14 22 A4
Sadlers Mead. SN15 23 E3
St Clements St. SN14 22 C3
St Francis Av. SN15 22 C5
St Josephs Dri. SN15 22 C5
St Lukes Dri. SN15 22 C5
St Margarets Gdns.
  SN15 22 C5
St Marys Pl. SN15 22 D3
St Mellion Clo. SN15 23 F4
St Paul St. SN15 22 D3
St Peters Clo. SN15 22 C5
St Teresa's Dri. SN15 22 C5
Salisbury Clo. SN14 22 A5
Saltersford La. SN14 22 A6
Sandes Clo. SN14 22 C4
Sandown Dri. SN14 22 A6
Sandpiper Gdns. SN14 22 A1
Sarum Rd. SN14 22 A5
Saxby Rd. SN15 23 E1
Saxon St. SN14 22 B3
School Walk. SN14 22 C4
Selions Clo. SN14 22 B1
Seymour Rd. SN15 23 F3
Sheeps Croft. SN14 22 B1
Sheldon Rd. SN14 22 B4
Silbury Clo. SN14 22 A6
Sorrel Dri. SN14 22 B1
Southmead. SN14 22 B5
Southwell Clo. SN14 22 A6
Spanbourn Av. SN15 22 B5
Spinney Clo. SN14 22 A5
Springfields Blds. SN15 22 A1
Stainers Way. SN14 22 A1
Station Hill. SN15 22 D3
Stockwood Rd. SN14 22 B5
Stonelea Clo. SN14 22 B4
Sunningdale Clo. SN15 23 F4
Sydney Wood Ct. SN14 22 D4
Tall Trees. SN15 22 D4
The Battens. SN14 22 A2
The Bridge. SN15 22 D4
The Butts. SN15 23 E5
The Cloisters. SN15 22 D5
The Firs. SN15 22 A5
The Hamlet. SN15 22 D2
The Oaks. SN15 22 D1
The Paddocks. SN15 23 E5
The Poplars. SN14 22 A2
The Tinings. SN15 23 F3
Thirsk Clo. SN14 22 A6
Timber St. SN15 23 E4
Timbrells Pl. SN15 22 C5
Torr Clo. SN14 22 B1

Truro Walk. SN14 22 A5
Tugela Rd. SN15 23 E2
Turnberry Clo. SN15 23 F4
Turpin Way. SN14 22 A4
Twickenham Way.
  SN15 23 E2
Union Rd. SN15 22 D3
Unity St. SN14 22 C4
Upper Farm Barns.
  SN14 22 B1
Utterson View. SN15 22 B1
Villiers Clo. SN15 23 F4
Vincients Rd. SN14 22 A2
Wardoar Rd. SN14 22 A5
Waters Edge. SN15 23 E6
Weavern Ct. SN14 22 A4
Webb Clo. SN15 23 E6
Webbington Rd. SN15 23 E6
Wedmore Av. SN15 22 C2
Wells Clo. SN14 22 A6
Wentworth Clo. SN15 23 F4
Wessex Rd. SN14 22 B3
West Cepen Way. SN14 22 A1
Westbrook Clo. SN14 22 A4
Westcroft. SN14 22 B6
Westerleigh Clo. SN14 22 B5
Westmead. SN15 22 D5
Westmead Ter. SN15 23 E5
Westminster Gdns.
  SN14 22 B4
Wetherby Clo. SN15 22 B4
Whittle Clo. SN14 22 A4
Wicks Dri. SN15 23 F6
Willow Gro. SN15 23 E1
Willowbank. SN14 22 B2
Winchester Clo. SN14 22 A5
Windlass Way. SN15 23 F6
Windsor Clo. SN14 22 A5
Wishart Way. SN15 23 F6
Wood La. SN15 23 E5
Woodlands Rd. SN14 22 C4
Woodpecker Mews.
  SN14 22 B1
Wyndham Clo. SN15 23 F3
Yewstock Cres East.
  SN15 22 C2
Yewstock Cres West.
  SN15 22 C2
York Clo. SN14 22 A5

CRICKLADE

Abingdon Ct La. SN6 26 C2
Bailiffs Piece. SN6 26 B1
Bath Ct. SN6 26 B2
Bath Rd. SN6 26 A2
Bishopsfields. SN6 26 A2
Branders. SN6 26 B1
Calcutt St. SN6 26 C2
Chelworth Rd. SN6 26 A3
Cherrytree Rd. SN6 26 B2
Church La. SN6 26 B2
Cirencester Rd. SN6 26 A2
Cliffords. SN6 26 A2
Common Hill. SN6 26 A2
Cricklade By-Pass. SN6 26 C1
Deansfield. SN6 26 B2
Doubledays. SN6 26 B2
Fairfield. SN6 26 B1
Fairview. SN6 26 C2
Fiddle Farm. SN6 26 A2
Foxleaze. SN6 26 B1
Fullers Av. SN6 26 B2
Galley Orchard. SN6 26 B2
Gas La. SN6 26 B2
Giles Av. SN6 26 B3
Hallsfield. SN6 26 A1
Hammonds. SN6 26 C2
High St. SN6 26 B2
Home Ground. SN6 26 A1
Hopkins Orchard. SN6 26 B2
Horse Fair La. SN6 26 B2
Keels. SN6 26 B1
Kitefield. SN6 26 B1
Lady Mead. SN6 26 A2
Malmesbury Rd. SN6 26 A2
Manor Orchard. SN6 26 A2
Middle Ground. SN6 26 A2
North Meadow Rd. SN6 26 A1
North Wall. SN6 26 B1
Ockwells. SN6 26 B3
Parsonage Farm La.
  SN6 26 B2
Pauls Croft. SN6 26 B3

Pike House Clo. SN6 26 A2
Pittsfield. SN6 26 B3
Pleydells. SN6 26 B1
Purton Rd. SN6 26 B2
Rectory La. SN6 26 C1
Red Lion La. SN6 26 C1
Reeds. SN6 26 A1
Saxon Clo. SN6 26 B3
Spital La. SN6 26 C2
Stones La. SN66 26 A2
Swindon Rd. SN6 26 C2
Thames Clo. SN6 26 C2
Thames La. SN6 26 B3
The Fiddle. SN6 26 A2
The Forty. SN6 26 B3
Water Furlong. SN6 26 B3
Waylands. SN6 26 A4
West Mill La. SN6 26 A1
White Horse Rd. SN6 26 B2

HIGHWORTH

Arran Way. SN6 4 A2
Barra Clo. SN6 4 A3
Biddel Springs. SN6 4 C3
Blandford Alley. SN6 4 B4
Botany. SN6 4 A4
Brewery St. SN6 4 C4
Brookfield. SN6 4 B2
Bute Clo. SN6 4 B2
Byde Mill Gdns. SN6 4 A4
Cherry Orchard. SN6 4 C3
Church Vw. SN6 4 B4
Crane Furlong. SN6 4 B2
Cricklade Rd. SN6 4 A4
Downs View. SN6 4 C3
Eastrop. SN6 4 C4
Edencroft. SN6 4 C2
Folly Clo. SN6 4 C2
Folly Cres. SN6 4 B2
Folly Dri. SN6 4 C2
Folly Way. SN6 4 C2
Grange Clo. SN6 4 C4
Grove Hill. SN6 4 B2
Grove Orchard. SN6 4 B2
Henley Dri. SN6 4 B2
High St. SN6 4 B4
Home Farm. SN6 4 A3
INDUSTRIAL ESTATES:
Blackworth Ind Est.
  SN6 4 B1
Islay Cres. SN6 4 B3
Kilda Rd. SN6 4 A2
Kings Av. SN6 4 C4
Knowlands. SN6 4 C2
Lechlade Rd. SN6 4 B4
Lismore Rd. SN6 4 A3
Market Pl. SN6 4 C3
Middi Haines Ct. SN6 4 C3
Newburgh Pl. SN6 4 B3
North Vw. SN6 4 B4
Oak Dri. SN6 4 B4
Orange Clo. SN6 4 C3
Park Av. SN6 4 C4
Parsonage Clo. SN6 4 C4
Pentylands Clo. SN6 4 B2
Pentlands La. SN6 4 B1
Pound Rd. SN6 4 B2
Priory Grn. SN6 4 C3
Quarry Cres. SN6 4 C2
Queens Av. SN6 4 C2
Rivers Pl. SN6 4 B3
Roman Way. SN6 4 A4
Round Hills Mead. SN6 4 C1
St Michaels Av. SN6 4 A3
Sevenfields. SN6 4 C2
Sheep St. SN6 4 C4
Shrivenham Rd. SN6 4 C5
Skye Clo. SN6 4 A2
Spa Clo. SN6 4 C3
Stapleton Clo. SN6 4 B4
Station Rd. SN6 4 B4
Stonefield Dri. SN6 4 B5
Stroma Way. SN6 4 B3
Swindon Rd. SN6 4 B6
Swindon St. SN6 4 B4
The Cullerns. SN6 4 C3
The Dormers. SN6 4 C4
The Elms. SN6 4 B4
The Green. SN6 4 B4
The Mews. SN6 4 C4
The Paddocks. SN6 4 C4
The Willows. SN6 4 C4
Turnpike Rd. SN6 4 C3

Vicarage La. SN6 4
Vorda Rd. SN6 4
Wessex Way. SN6 4
Westhill Clo. SN6 4
Westrop. SN6 4
Windrush. SN6 4
Wrde Hill. SN6 4

MARLBOROUGH

Alexandra Ter. SN8 24 D
Alma Pl. SN8 24 D
Angel Yd. SN8 24 D
Aubrey Clo. SN8 24 B
Back La. SN8 24 C
Bailey Acre. SN8 24 D
Barn St. SN8 24 D
Barnfield. SN8 25 G
Barrow Clo. SN8 25 F
Bath Rd. SN8 24 A
Bay Water Vw. SN8 24 D
Baybridge. SN8 25 F
Benson Clo. SN8 24 B
Betjeman Rd. SN8 24 A
Blackwell Path. SN8 24 D
Blowhorn St. SN8 24 D
Bridewell St. SN8 24 C
Bridge St. SN8 24 A
Cardigan Rd. SN8 24 C
Chantry La. SN8 24 D
Cherry Orchard. SN8 25 E
Chestnut Dri. SN8 24 D
Chopping Knife La.
  SN8 25 G
Cold Harbour La. SN8 24 D
College Fields. SN8 25 E
Copes Yd. SN8 25 E
Cross La. SN8 24 C
Culvermead Clo. SN8 25 E
Dando Dri. SN8 24 B
Davies Clo. SN8 24 A
Ducks Meadow. SN8 24 D
Edwards Mdw. SN8 24 B
Elcot Clo. SN8 25 F
Elcot La. SN8 25 F
Elcot Orchard. SN8 25 G
Falkner Clo. SN8 24 B
Farrar Dri. SN8 24 A
Figgins La. SN8 24 D
Five Stiles Rd. SN8 25 F
Francklyn Acre. SN8 24 D
Frees Av. SN8 24 B
Gales Grd. SN8 25 E
George La. SN8 24 D
Golding Av. SN8 24 A
Grand Av. SN8 25 H
Granham Clo. SN8 24 C
Granham Hill. SN8 24 C
Hawkins Meadow. SN8 24 B
Hazel Clo. SN8 25 G
Herd St. SN8 24 D
High St, Manton. SN8 24 A
High St,
  Marlborough. SN8 24 D
Hilliers Yd. SN8 24 D
Homefields. SN8 25 F
Hughenden Yd. SN8 24 A
Hughes Clo. SN8 24 A
Hyde La. SN8 24 C
Ironmonger La. SN8 24 D
Irving Way. SN8 24 C
Isbury La. SN8 24 D
Isbury Rd. SN8 24 D
Jefferies Clo. SN8 24 B
Kennet Mews. SN8 24 D
Kennet Pl. SN8 24 D
Kingsbury St. SN8 24 C
Lainey's Clo. SN8 24 D
Laurel Dri. SN8 25 F
Lawrence Acre. SN8 24 D
Leaf Clo. SN8 25 E
Leaze Rd. SN8 25 E
London Rd. SN8 25 E
Lower Church Fld. SN8 24 D
Lyne's View. SN8 24 C
MacNeice Dri. SN8 24 A
Manton Drove. SN8 24 A
Manton Hollow. SN8 24 A
Mayfield. SN8 25 E
Morris Rd. SN8 24 B
New Rd. SN8 24 D
Newby Acre. SN8 24 D
North View Pl. SN8 24 D